A child so innocent.

A Life Hidden from View

Why did this happen to an innocent child?

By
I Walsh

Grosvenor House
Publishing Limited

This book is published by
Grosvenor House Publishing Ltd
Link House
140 The Broadway, Tolworth, Surrey, KT6 7HT.
www.grosvenorhousepublishing.co.uk

A CIP record for this book
is available from the British Library

ISBN 978-1-80381-207-6
eBook ISBN 978-1-80381-243-4

Disclaimer: "This book is a memoir. It reflects its author's recollections
of experiences. The author has changed the names and characteristics
of many individuals and organisations to protect their privacy.
Where the names of individuals, organisations, businesses, places or
events are used, they are/may be fictional, and any resemblance to
an actual person, living or dead, or actual events is purely co-incidental."

Life

Can be unpredictable…
All the gears are in one box
Sort them out

CONTENTS

CHAPTER 1

THE EARLY YEARS

Oh, Mother, what have you done? Bringing shame into the family and farming community. Our lovely harmonious, rural sleepy village will never be the same again.

I was born into a somewhat dysfunctional family. I shared our home with my mother Florence, who was never cut out to be a mother at all (honestly, some women should keep their legs crossed!), two of her sisters, Hilda and Elizabeth, and my maternal grandparents, John and Margaret. After my birth, which apparently was a bit traumatic for my mother, she brought me back home to the family house – an old property called Rose Hill Cottage. I don't remember it myself, as I was about three years old when we moved out. My mother would talk about her favourite cat Fluffy, who used to sit at the gate waiting for her to come home from work, but she never talked about me. So, I have no idea what my day consisted of during those very early years. Until clearing my mother's house years later, I found some photos of me as a young child.

I have been told that the cottage was surrounded by an orchard, with the odd hen cabin dotted around, and Grandfather was always chasing off passers-by who sneaked into the orchard to steal apples. My Great Uncle Ivor came daily to look after the hens and had a gorgeous light brown and white collie dog called

Lassie, like the one in the film. On one dark stormy night, the wind brought the chimney stack crashing down straight through the roof, so we had to make a hasty exit from that property. There was an empty farmhouse further down the road, which we could move into. The property had no electricity, only cold water on tap and basic toilet facilities. All the ground floor rooms had flagstone floors, whitewashed walls; only the living room had lino and coconut matting to walk on, the rest were just bare stone floors. We had a coal fire where you would always find a kettle bubbling away on the grate, and an oven to the side, although I can't recall the oven ever being used for baking. We had paraffin lamps and candles to light the way and oil stoves for cooking. There was a pantry with shelving where we kept our food.

There was only one door to enter the property, which was at the back as you entered; the stairs were immediately facing you, living room was to the right, and the kitchen to the left. The kitchen had a big boiler, underneath was a coal fire to heat the water for washing and bathing. There were several oil heaters for cooking, an old sink with a rattly cold-water tap, and a few cupboards containing pots, pans, and crockery.

There was another room just off the living room, which my grandparents used for their bedroom. I don't remember going into this room much, because my grandmother was ill and spent a lot of her time there, and maybe it was thought that I would annoy her.

Upstairs we had four bedrooms – whitewashed walls, lino to the floors, and a peg rug beside our beds, possibly made by Aunt Hilda. She loved making them and would sit cutting up our old clothes into tiny strips, then weaving these pieces in and out of her backing cloth. We all had a chamber pot under our beds, as the toilet was right at the bottom of the garden. It was my job to cut up the newspaper and string it up next to the toilet when I was old enough. I imagine we all had black bottoms from the ink. Then along came Izal toilet paper.

During the winter months we all had hot water bottles to warm our beds, but as I remember our bed mattresses and pillows were filled with a mixture of flock and horsehair. They were warm when you had sunk into the middle of them – I guess the original version of today's memory foam mattresses. Bath night was a tin bath in front of the fire in the living room. Friday was my bath night, which I liked, especially when my mother washed my hair. I used to like her pouring the water over my head to rinse the soap out. But my mother would get me into the bath by the fire, just as relatives were due to visit. Every week she did this and I remember crying while they all watched me get bathed, I was so shy. This took all the enjoyment out of it for me. My mother hadn't the sense to bath me at a different time of night. Equally, our visitors could have come at a different time. I must have provided a lot of entertainment, to my embarrassment.

Speaking of entertainment, we mainly made our own. As a small child, I learnt to read quite well at a young age, as we would all sit around the coal fire of an evening and I would read books to the rest of my family. We did have a radio that had an accumulator, and my family would gather around it to listen to their favourite programmes and the news.

Even though times were difficult, and my family worked very hard, we did have a great sense of humour and fun. We all loved taking the mickey out of each other, and out of strangers sometimes. We all loved comedy, listening to radio shows to hear the comedians of the day who made us laugh. On one occasion, Aunt Liz was expecting someone to call round. She had cut a face of someone out of a paper, and when there was a knock at the door, she opened it and thrust the picture into their face, and said, 'Kissy, kissy.' Unfortunately, it wasn't who she was expecting, but the insurance man! In those days we had various tradespeople calling: bread man; fish man; grocer; coal man. Most things you could buy at your door, and we also had the travelling salesmen who came round door-to-door with their suitcases full of odds and ends. When you opened the door to them, they would always put their case down over the door frame to stop you shutting the door in their face. We also had the gypsies calling with their 'lucky heather'.

My mother was the youngest of four girls, and she worked in a sweet factory in our local town until she was called up to serve in the WRAF during the Second World War. By all accounts, she enjoyed her time away serving her country (well, looking after the airmen, to be precise; she was a cook!). I hope they put her on washing-up duties, as she made terrible chips for us at home. She made friends and got to see more of our country, which made her into a more confident person. When she came home on leave, she and the other officers would bring some food with them to help out while they were back at home, so the families had a little bit extra to go with their meagre rations. When she came home after the war, she went back to work in the sweet factory, but more on her terms. She didn't let her boss order her around anymore.

Audrey, the next youngest sister, married and went to live down south.

Hilda, the next to eldest sister, was a home bird and worked mainly as a housekeeper for a local vegetable producer, John Wright, who had a smallholding in the village where he grew a variety of vegetables and flowers for the market. When Hilda wasn't cooking and cleaning for him, she was working out in the fields picking vegetables and bunching flowers. When John died, Hilda went to work as a cleaner and carer in a nursing home in the town, which was reputed to be haunted. She hated anything to do with spirits, and we used to torment her a lot about it. If, as a family, we were talking about death, ghosts, or the supernatural, you would soon see Aunt Hilda slope off into another room. As time went on, she developed rheumatoid arthritis which crippled her whole body, so she had to retire from work. She suffered greatly from this, but she never once complained.

In later years, Mum and I would visit Elizabeth and Hilda once a week. The last time I saw Hilda, as I was leaving, a strange thing happened. She turned around in her chair and had a good look at me and said, 'Goodbye.' Normally, her arthritis wouldn't have allowed her body to do that; it must have been so painful for her. A few days later, she passed away. A few memories that have stuck in my mind of Aunt Hilda are that, unlike the rest of us, she had lovely thick hair and would spend hours brushing it. She also used to sneak into her bedroom to eat oranges – I don't think she wanted to share them with the rest of us. She was also pedantic about wearing clothes for the seasons, instead of wearing according to the weather. On the 1st of May every year, her dresses would come out; it could be snowing, but she had to wear a dress. I can still hear her now saying, 'I will starve it out.' Mum and I have always blamed this for her developing her arthritis.

Elizabeth, the eldest sister, again was a home bird. As a young girl, she took on the role of housekeeper at home because her mother was ill, and she looked after her three younger siblings. When her sisters were old enough to look after themselves, Elizabeth got a job working full-time in a factory, washing and packing vegetables for the retail trade. I never knew her to work anywhere else. She was a very well-respected employee, and when she died the owner of the factory attended her funeral and gave a lovely eulogy. Memories I have of Aunt Liz were that she used to bleach her hair, and she was always very slim, when the rest of us tend to be all 'belly and bum'. She used to drink undiluted PLJ, which she did for years as she believed it kept her complexion clear. She didn't want rosy cheeks. (Aunt Hilda had rosy cheeks!) In later life, she developed oesophageal cancer which we put down to her drinking the PLJ without diluting it. When she was diagnosed with this, she was sent into Hospital for an experimental operation to remove her oesophagus, attaching her stomach to her throat, but she didn't survive the operation. The saddest thing as we sat with her as she passed away was that her body was bloated and her face very red; she would have hated that. This was in 1979 but thank goodness treatments have improved.

It was a lovely summer's day back in 1979 and my Aunt Liz had recently passed away. Every Sunday I took Mum to the crematorium to put some flowers where her ashes had been buried. This particular Sunday, I was driving my old Ford Fiesta down the main road towards the crematorium, chatting away to Mum and occasionally glancing towards her as she sat in the passenger seat. At one point, I glanced toward her and 'she had gone'. I discovered she was lying flat; the back rest of her seat had broken and she ended up with her head resting on the back seat. When I enquired why she had not said anything, she replied, 'Well, I didn't want you to take your eyes off the road.' I offered to pull over so she could get out and sit in the back, but she replied, 'Don't worry, we are nearly there, and I am not uncomfortable.' So, we arrived at the crematorium and parked up a couple of spaces from a red Mini, with a very elderly couple sitting inside busy tucking into their 'butties' and pouring a drink from a flask. I got out of the car and went round to the passenger side to open the door for my mum, but unfortunately, she could not get herself up from her lying position. As I proceeded to help her out, I just happened to glance at the elderly couple. They watched me half lifting, half dragging Mum out of the car, and the look of sheer horror on their faces was a picture. I can only imagine what they were thinking, but I suspect they thought I had brought a dead body.

I don't have many recollections about Grandmother Margaret, as she died when I was eight, and was totally bedridden during most of those years. She had been a typical housewife but became ill at a young age with cancer. She must have been a tough old bird as she lived until 73 years of age, suffering with the disease for many years, and from what I have learnt she would not even take a painkiller. When the family doctor visited, he would offer her pain relief but she always refused. She used to say, 'He's trying to kill me.' So, I was told.

Grandfather John…now then, there is a little mystery surrounding him. My mother always said he came over from Ireland looking for work, but we have never been able to substantiate this. On doing some research and chatting with a family member who is preparing a family tree, it appears that he came from Liverpool. He worked the land with a horse and plough for the farmer who owned the farmhouse we lived in, so we were allowed to live there rent-free because he worked the land, but he got very little pay as a result. Over the years he had several horses to work with. Jack, his favourite, was a gentle and stunning dark bay horse who was very well loved and looked after by Grandad. (He cared very much for all the horses he worked with.) When they were coming back to the stable after a hard day's work, Grandad would take off Jack's bridle so he could have a good drink from the water trough, then Jack would head to the kitchen window, stick his head in for his treat – eggs – or he would raid the hens' nests in his stable and eat the eggs. These eggs were left for Jack, and he had a lovely glossy coat as a result.

When Grandad was nearing retirement, he was given a young horse who was just too fast and lively for him to keep up with.

I think this went a long way to shortening Grandad's life, and at 69 years of age he collapsed while collecting his pension at the Post Office and never recovered. Bless him, he didn't get much retirement to enjoy, just a few weeks. On that day, my mother told me that Grandad got washed and changed before going for his pension – something he had never done before. Mum thought he must have known this was the end. Grandad and Grandma died two months apart, in 1957. On the day Grandma died, she told my mother that John had spent the night with her. My memories of Grandad are that he would sit in the living room next to the fire, still wearing his cap, smoking a pipe, and he would spit into the fire. Being on a farm, we had quite a few cats, mainly to keep the mice down in the outbuildings – the barn especially. One of the cats came into the house, and Grandad would take his cap off and put it on his knee, so the cat would jump up and sit in his cap. Most of the other cats stayed outside, only coming to the door to be fed.

When Grandad died, the family had his body brought to the house, and he was laid resting in his bedroom. Because he had been well looked after by the Funeral Directors and made to look very much at peace, as though he was just sleeping, my mother decided I could go in and look at him. I did several times. I'm not sure I really understood, but he looked nice in his white gown with a net gauze over his face, which I kept lifting up to touch him and to say goodbye. I do remember a slight odour, but it wasn't overpowering. My grandmother's bed was moved out of this room at the time.

When my grandmother died, it was a different matter. She had suffered terribly with stomach cancer, and when one of my Great Aunts came round to help my mother to lay her out, her back was raw with the cancer. It broke their hearts, as she had never once had any pain relief nor complained. As it was obvious to my mother that she had died in pain (it showed on her face), I wasn't allowed to see her. I do wish I had been able to have more time with my grandparents, as I know very little about them.

In those days, people generally took out an insurance to pay for their funerals, and both my grandparents had done this, so it enabled them to have the best solid oak coffins available at the time and a good headstone. Nowadays you can take out a modern-style Funeral Plan, but they are restrictive. I still believe that saving for your funeral is the best option.

My mother came back from her time away during the Second World War and settled back into her old job at the Sweet Factory but left a few years later. After a while, she found herself pregnant. I don't know why she didn't stay at home during her confinement. By this time, she was working for our family doctor, so he arranged for her to go down south and work for a colleague of his until I was born. She went to live with her sister Audrey, and I have learned that I was born in her home. My mother was not a great one for talking and she never spoke to me about her reason for doing this. Nor did she ever tell me who my biological father was. But I have always wondered and wanted to know who he was. My family either kept all this information as a guarded secret, or my mother never even told them. I guess it's the latter. But I did track him down later in life.

I recall on one occasion my mother telling me that when she was expecting me, she hoped I didn't have a big nose and/or big ears. I spent a lot of time looking through old photos of my mother's and thinking back to men who may have been in her life at the time I was born but drawn a blank. I could have family members out there, whereas nearly all the family on my mother's side have now passed away. So, during my retirement, I have set about trying to find out who he was.

One day I popped into the world. I have been told I was born at my Aunt Audrey's house, and it was suggested to my mother that she leave me with them. But my mother didn't take up that offer and eventually took me back home to her parents and sisters. I'm not sure how old I was, maybe a few weeks, as there are old photographs of my grandmother and grandfather holding me at just a few months old.

My mother would have to go out to work to support us, so I assume that Grandma looked after me, as she was still well enough at times to get around then, and Aunt Hilda only worked part-time so maybe she took on some of my caring duties. Aunt Hilda seemed to be fond of me. As I got older, she used to take me outside every night before bed to look at the stars – apparently, they fascinated me – and to listen to our lovely Barn Owl. Later on, during my research, I found out that Aunt Hilda was one of my godparents.

It wasn't long before it became common knowledge in our village that Florence had had a baby out of wedlock, and it became evident that some people in the village gave us a wide berth and stopped speaking to us. Others just accepted me for who I was and didn't judge.

As the months went by, and I grew into a toddler, my mother was not happy that she was 'lumbered' with a child. She would complain that she couldn't go out socializing and meeting up with friends as she used to do. She had a very good friend, who she went out with in the evenings – usually to a local pub, where they would order two ciders. One evening as they entered the pub, walking towards the bar, they heard one of the bar staff comment, 'Here come the two ciders.' They never went in that pub again.

I digress. Her parents were very strict, especially Grandad. He made her stay at home and look after her child. When I was older, he was strict with me, too. On one occasion when I had been naughty, he chased me round the sofa till he caught me, then off came his belt and he whipped me with the buckle end. It worked. I don't remember ever being naughty again. That is when things started to get difficult for me. As soon as I could sit up on my own properly, my mother left me sitting on the cold flagstone floor in the kitchen while they all went out to work. She told me years later that I was so stupid that when she got home from work, I was still sitting in the same spot; I hadn't moved, or crawled anywhere, as a normal baby would. Maybe I was too cold to move. Certainly, Grandma wasn't always well enough to care for me.

My Great Aunt Harriet and Great Uncle Ivor lived in the village. They had a smallholding where they kept hens and grew produce, and my mother would often 'pawn' me off on them. Aunt Harriet would take me with her into the fields while she was working, and I was left sitting in a cold wheelbarrow, open to all the elements.

As a result, I became very poorly. My mother didn't seem to bother and apparently just left me in my cot without any proper care. Eventually, our family doctor was called and he and his wife took me and nursed me back to health, but I was left with a weak bladder and kidneys. As I got better, I was taken back home, and at Christmas time, Dr Harrison and his wife turned up at our farmhouse with a huge, real Christmas tree. Mrs Harrison propped me up in a chair so that I could watch Dr Harrison put up the tree, which touched the ceiling. She had brought a box of decorations, and I watched her dressing the tree. It was magical to me; we hadn't had a Christmas tree before.

As years passed, in many ways it was an idyllic life for a young child to live on a farm out in the middle of nowhere. The farmhouse and outbuildings were places for me to explore and let my imagination run wild. I have always been a dreamer. The farmhouse was surrounded by orchards, gardens, and fields, so as a child growing up, I had plenty of room to play. At the front of the farmhouse was a large, grassed area, planted with hundreds of daffodil bulbs, as was the side orchard, along with apple and pear trees. They looked stunning in Spring. Next door was the Methodist Chapel, where Mr Abbot was the Minister. On the days that the ladies came to work in the Chapel, I would squeeze through the hedge and go and join them. I imagine I made more of a nuisance of myself rather than anything else, but they tolerated me. I suppose, like a lot of people, they would quiz me about my family situation, to my mother's annoyance.

Worshippers would come on a Sunday and, following the service, some would knock on our door and ask to buy the flowers which my aunts had picked and bunched the previous day and stored in the understairs cupboard in the dark so the buds wouldn't open to early. We also got people just driving past, who would stop and come and ask for some flowers.

When Mr Abbot died, his funeral was held at the Chapel. I watched his cortege arrive and the pallbearers carrying his coffin shoulder-high into the Chapel. As he was carried down the long drive, I concentrated on his coffin. Suddenly I saw an arm flung out from under the lid and it had a black jacket sleeve on. Even then, at such a young age, I seemed to have the ability to link into the spirit world, which will be covered in a later chapter.

Across the yard from the back of the house was the washhouse. I remember the mangle being in there, which would be used every Monday – wash day (rain or shine). There was a boiler in the kitchen, and the water in this was heated by a coal fire underneath it. The cotton clothes were put in to boil before being washed in a Dolly Tub with Dolly Legs. The Dolly Legs were manually swirled about in the same manner as today's automatic washing machines, then the clothes were moved from one tub to another for rinsing, using wooden tongs, A Dolly Blue tablet was added to keep the whites white, and then the aprons would be starched.

Behind the washhouse was our garden, where all our vegetables and some flowers were grown. Further along the path was the outside toilet. Growing at the side of this building was a lilac tree, and over the years the branches grew over the roof, eventually encapsulating the whole toilet building. In Spring the whole tree was covered with gorgeous lilac blooms, which gave off a real heady scent – probably masking the smell from the toilet. Lilac was my mother's favourite colour and flower, though she also loved Lily of the Valley. On one occasion I bought her a lilac floral dress for a birthday and she wore it a lot. I digress! This toilet building was adjoined onto what was an old pigsty, which was always empty as we didn't keep pigs. Beyond that was a field surrounded by hedges. This is where we had our washing line; on wet days the washing was hung up in the washhouse to dry.

Joined onto the house were the outbuildings and stables, and at the end of the large drive was the barn, which was filled with bales of straw. As I got a bit older, my friends and I had great fun playing among the bales. We would climb up to the top of the stack, then find a gap and slide back down to the bottom, never thinking that the whole lot could come down on top of us. In another crazy game we played, we climbed up the ladder to the first floor of one of the outbuildings and then jumped off into a small pile of hay. Looking back, we could have broken our necks. The stables were originally used to stable the horses that Grandad worked with, but later they just lay empty, I spent many hours playing there with my imaginary horses. I would make saddles out of sacks stuffed with straw, bridles and stirrups made out of string. Most of the other outbuildings were empty, but for a while a local farmer used a few of them for his cattle. I remember a bull being in one of them at one time, but I was told to stay away from it, as it wasn't a friendly animal.

The friends I made from the surrounding area all lived in houses with electricity and televisions. When I went to play with them at their houses, I did watch a bit of TV, but I wasn't really bothered then about sitting down and watching something on a TV set. I would much rather be outside in the fresh air.

Between our farmhouse and my Great Aunt Harriet's house were two fields. The first one, next to the Methodist Chapel, always had a few horses in, but I never knew who they belonged to. The horses had a habit of getting out and running free in the cultivated fields over the road. The next field usually had two cattle in; I think they were a pedigree, as I remember they were all grey. I hadn't seen cattle that colour before, nor since, and the chap that owned them bred from them. I found it very scary walking past that field, as the fence was so flimsy, and the bull would charge at anyone walking past, especially if they had a calf in the field with them.

The couple who owned this property, land, and the cattle, were very good to me. I became very friendly with their daughter Susie and went regularly to play with her. If Susie's mother was going out, she would of course take Susie with her, and if I was round playing, she would bundle me in the car as well and take me along. She was a lovely lady; I liked her a lot. I was never sure exactly what Susie's dad did for a living, as he was away from home quite a bit. I remember seeing him driving large lorries in and out of his drive, but what he did bring home were large jars of sweets – well, at least Susie and I thought they were sweets, as we used to creep up into the hay loft area of their barn where the jars were stashed and open them and eat some. They were not very nice.

Another good friend I had was Denise. We were in the same class at school, and her mum used to take me along with her children on days out during school holidays as well. Because all my family worked, during the holidays I was shut out of the house and just left to play and amuse myself, so I think Denise's mum took pity on me. My mother didn't like it, because I would be in my dirty play clothes. On one occasion when I was at Denise's house, her mother was playing with her children and hugging them. As I sat and observed this, I was thinking, what is she doing? My mother doesn't behave like that. Spending so much time on my own, I think this is where I gained my ability to always be thinking up things to do. Even now, as I am older, I still have an active brain and always like to have a project on the go.

On the occasions that I was ill, I would be left in the farmhouse in bed on my own, the house locked until my mother came home from work. Thankfully, at that time she had several part-time jobs, so I would sit on the bed looking out through the window waiting for the bus to come round the 'sticks' (a very narrow winding road), as we nicknamed it. Once home, my mother would light the coal fire, but I still wasn't allowed to go downstairs until the room had warmed a bit. How ironic, after being left in a freezing cold bedroom all morning.

My mother's ritual every lunchtime when she got back from work was to light the fire, then make some lunch. We had a blue budgie called Joey at the time; his cage was hung from the ceiling to keep him away from the cats. At lunchtime, his cage was brought down, put on the table and his door opened, so he could have a fly around. My mother also put a saucer of water on the table, and he loved to splash about in it.

On one occasion when I had the measles, I had to be moved into my mother's bedroom, as she had a working coal fire in hers; doctor's orders, I had to be kept warm. As my mother arrived for work on one of these mornings – she was working for our family doctor, Dr Harrison, cleaning the surgery – and apparently, he told her off for leaving me alone in the house. He sent her home with strict instructions not to go back to work until I was back at school.

Having all the surrounding fields and woods to play in with my friends, we never felt we were in any danger. We would on occasions come across a 'tramp' who was stealing potatoes and vegetables from the fields. They would later turn up at our door, asking us to cook what they had taken, and in turn they would do a few odd jobs for us. Then they bedded down for the night in the barn. This worried my mother in case they set fire to the bales of straw as they smoked their pipes or cigarettes. We loved the harvest time, when the corn was cut and made into sheaves, then stacked up like wigwams. They were great for playing hide and seek.

When the farmers were harvesting the vegetables, at the end of the day they drove the tractor and cart back to base, loaded up with what they had picked that day – could be carrots, peas, cabbages, or potatoes – and they stopped by our gate and threw some off down the path for us. We did grow a few veg ourselves, but this helped us out a lot.

We all got around on bicycles, young and old; no-one had cars, apart from the better-off farmers and the landed gentry from the Mansion House. I loved my bike, as it was different to my friends. Mine had a back-pedal brake, while my friends' bikes had their brakes activated by a lever on the handlebars.

Growing up, I developed a love of horses. I don't know where that came from, as there have not been any horsey people in our family, apart from Grandad, but he never rode them. They had some gorgeous horses up at the Mansion House, and the family went hunting and competing on them at shows. For a while I was friends with a young girl who lived up there. She rode, but I was never allowed anywhere near the horses in case I got hurt.

My family were quite religious, so Sundays for me meant Sunday School in the mornings and Evensong with the family in the evenings. Our family church, St Nicholas, was quite a distance from the farm but there was a Mission Hut in the village, and we would get lay preachers coming on a Sunday to give the services. A girl who was ten years older than me would play the piano, so we could sing hymns. We built up a friendship, but as she was older, we eventually went our separate ways. I did have my confirmation at St Nicholas when the Canon Fairbrother came to officiate. When we moved into the cottage, though, we stopped going to church, and I only restarted in 2010 after my mother died. I started attending a local Methodist Chapel and made some good friends there.

Sundays for us also meant a nice family meal – Sunday roast, with Grandad mopping up all the left-over fat with slices of bread. We usually had fruit and jelly after. I would only eat red jelly, or so I thought. When Mum had made a lemon or lime jelly, she put mine in a red dish so that I would eat it. My mother also made ginger beer, as a friend had given her some root ginger. I was allowed a glass of this on a Sunday with all the adults. She made this for several years, and the bottles were stored in our cold pantry. One night, as we sat round the fire, we heard corks popping and bottles exploding.

I was given packets and packets of Rolos from the farm workers, but now I really wish they hadn't. They weren't good for my teeth, and I had many fillings at a young age. Surprisingly, I still have my own teeth, albeit most of them have been filled.

A few years after losing both my grandparents, we had to leave the farmhouse and we moved into a cottage further out on the outskirts of the village. Compared to the farmhouse, it was a small property, two up, two down, with a couple of outbuildings and a coal store on the end. We had electricity in this place but still no hot running water. There were four of us initially sharing two bedrooms. I shared a room with my mother; Aunt Hilda had the other upstairs room; and Aunt Liz used the front room as her bedroom. I didn't like the stairs as they were very steep, always seemed a bit rickety, and creaked a lot. We rented this property from the landlord who lived next door with his brother.

CHAPTER 2

OFF TO SCHOOL

I started school at the age of five, at Carstairs School which was, and still is, a church school associated with St Nicholas. The school building was all on one level with all the classrooms surrounding a central area, which I can only remember as a large, squarish space with wooden floor, windows all around three sides, giving visual access to all the classrooms. I don't think this area was used for anything other than giving access to all the rooms. On the other side of the building were two entrances, which led into a cloakroom and washroom; we hung our coats and satchels in there. Leading off one of the washrooms was the teachers' staff room. We had a separate building with a stage and this room was very well used, as we had assembly in the mornings, then it was set up for our school dinners at lunchtime. At other times all the sports equipment would be brought in (that dreaded wooden horse!), although the climbing frames up the walls were a permanent feature. We also used this room for our dancing lessons, and at Christmas time we performed our Nativity on the stage, while on the last day of school we had our annual party.

All the area around the school building was tarmac, except for a small, grassed area right at the back perimeter of the playground. It was okay to play on, so long as you didn't fall over. I did on one occasion and landed on a rusty nail. The school nurse and a teacher took me into the nurse's room, where they deliberated as to whether a plaster would suffice, or I needed to go and have stitches. They decided on a plaster, and I still have a scar on my knee. The toilets were quite a way from the main school building, at the front, next to the caretaker's workshop. Mr Roberts looked after the garden area and kept everything else running smoothly. At the other side of his workshop were the kitchens, where the ladies made our dinners. For a while I was given a packed lunch by my mother, which consisted of syrup butties every day, and by the time lunchtime arrived my 'butties' were all soggy. I was glad to eventually get free school dinners; they were not great, but better than syrup butties. (What with those butties and Rolos, I am lucky to still have any teeth!)

I was picked up for school by the school bus, and I remember being so scared and crying my eyes out even before I had got on board. The coach picked up children for drop-off at various schools on the route to Carstairs. After we had moved to the cottage, the bus would stop outside our house to pick me up. Some friends lived at a farm just down the road. One day when the bus was bringing us home from school, it stopped outside their farm and they got off the bus, but the youngest member ran across the road towards her house and was hit by a speeding car. She died later in hospital. She was only six years old, one of five siblings. A few weeks later one of her sisters told me, when they were playing out in the garden, their late sister appeared and joined in the game. That road is very long and straight, with no road markings, and was used as a racetrack by a lot of drivers. It's no better today. On each side of the narrow road are deep ditches, and many vehicles have ended up in them.

I was used to buses because Mum took me to town with her on a Saturday shopping, and we always went by bus. But on this occasion, perhaps I thought Mum was sending me off on a bus on my own to get rid of me.

My infant class teacher Miss Roby was an older lady. I don't really remember much about being in the infants from an education point of view, probably because I cried all the time. But I do remember those warm bottles of milk we were given to drink; I cannot drink milk now, as that put me off for life. All the children in class took turns at being milk monitor. I recall a time when I got a spanking. Possibly because I needed the toilet, I got out of my seat and walked to the front of the class. Miss Roby has disappeared behind a screen, and when I stuck my head around it, there she was fixing her suspender. There was a lad in my class who was very overweight, he always had a bright red face and he had a habit of projectile vomiting just out of the blue. He was always doing it. Now as an adult, looking back, I think he must have had something wrong with him. Maybe that's when my vomit phobia started.

As I moved up through the classes, the bullying started from the other children when they discovered I came from an illegitimate family. During those years there was only one other little girl who didn't have a father at home. Her dad was in prison, so we both got stick, but for me it was much worse. I remember each playtime just running into the toilets, locking myself in a cubicle, crying and waiting for the bell to go back to class. All the time other children were banging on the toilet door calling me names. I soon found out that parents of some of the other children had told them not to speak to me, which just ignited the fire in the children to bully me more. So, no surprise I hated school and didn't really try to learn anything. I just didn't want to be there. I do wish now that I could have found the strength within me to fight back, as you only get one chance at an education and I let mine slip through my fingers. On reflection, if I had worked hard, I could have made something of myself; a life wasted. But because of my isolated way of life, I never learnt how to interact with others.

On occasions I would ask my mum, 'Why do I not have a daddy, like the other children at school?' My mother would get angry with me and tell me to 'stop asking'. So, in the end, I just gave up.

My first move to another class was to Miss Bamber's class. Here we had more structured learning, with the basics of English, maths, and a lot of Scripture in that class, but this was not continued up the years.

When I moved into Mr Abram's class, we started doing technical drawing. I liked that and appeared to be quite good at it, although I still cannot draw freehand. One thing sticks in my mind about this class. Our school was mixed and there was one lad, who shall remain nameless, who was always getting his 'willy' out and showing everyone, then playing with it, in a childlike way. That's one drawback to young lads wearing short trousers.

I think it was around this time, as I was growing up, that I started giggling in class – quite regularly, as I recall. I was made to stand in the corner many, many times for giggling for no apparent reason. I also got the ruler across my knuckles.

Miss Pierce was the youngest teacher at the school and in her class, we did cookery and sewing. I wasn't good at sewing and didn't enjoy it but wasn't bad at cookery. At that time the boys could choose either cookery or woodwork. We had just one lad in our cookery class, and he provided a bit of entertainment for us girls, but he was actually good at it. His *piece de resistance* was showing off that he could crack the egg into the bowl using just one hand and not getting any shell into the mixture. A professional chef in the making, I think.

On one occasion when it was Great Aunt Harriet and Uncle Ivor's wedding anniversary, I decided to bake them a cake at home. I made a fruit cake, iced it, and decorated it with those little silver balls. I took it round to their house and Aunt Harriet was thrilled with it. As all my family were out when I got home from school, I used to go round to Aunt Harriet's to watch a bit of TV. If Aunt Harriet had been baking, she always left me the bowl to scrape out, and I loved that. Maybe she was the one who gave me an interest in baking. A few days before the anniversary, some visitors arrived unexpectedly and Aunt Harriet didn't have anything to offer these visitors with a cup of tea, so she cut into my cake. My mother was not happy about this at all. Aunt Harriet really tried to persuade me when I left school to go and train as a confectioner, but my mother was having none of it. She wanted me earning.

In the music class, our teacher was Miss Openshaw – another quite older lady. As the instruments were allocated, I was given the triangle. As I am tone deaf and don't have a musical note in my body, I think she chose wisely. I didn't enjoy music lessons.

Mr Grundy was the headmaster; I can't recall him ever teaching a class I was in, but maybe he taught the older children. A Mr Briggs joined the staff, but I don't remember him teaching us either. Maybe he came to teach the sixth form, as we didn't automatically sit for exams. We had to be invited to stay on in the sixth form to do O Levels, and only the brightest pupils got invited. Mr Briggs was a handsome young man, and I think he had many girls experiencing their first man crush.

When it came to PE, some things I liked, others not. I couldn't cope with that wooden vaulting horse and I used to keep creeping to the back of the queue so that I never got a turn. But I loved the sack race on sports day, as one of the workers on the farm used to give me a chaff sack – larger than an average sack – so when I had my feet in the corners, I could run faster. I did win the sack race, and I wasn't bad at the general running races either.

I didn't excel at any ball games, rounders, and the like. I think my co-ordination must be poor. Trying to play badminton or tennis, I could never hit the ball or shuttlecock.

We did have swimming lessons, and I enjoyed these as it meant some time out of school. We went once a week by coach to the local swimming baths. I can remember being fastened to a long rope at first but was soon doing handstands all by myself. I didn't mind getting my head under the water. Once these classes finished, I didn't continue learning to swim, but started again when I was in my forties.

I enjoyed the dancing lessons – mainly we did barn dancing, which was fun. We used to have an annual dance where we all dressed up, so my mother and a friend of hers took me into the city to look for a dress. She bought me a pink, frilly satin little number and a pair of silver shoes.

When I had just one more year to do at school, the powers-that-be decided to turn the school into just a primary, so it meant that all the children from the age of 12 up had to leave and go to a neighbouring Secondary Modern School. Thankfully, I only had one year to go there. But I didn't see a great lot of it, as I played truant a lot with a friend because we both hated it.

We arrived at the secondary school in September and were allocated to our new classes. It was a bit odd on both sides, because none of us wanted to go there and no-one wanted us there. It took a long while for us all to settle.

It felt more institutionalised compared to the Carstairs school, which was more open and airier. All the corridors circled a concrete quadrangle, which did have some trees to break up the harshness of the concrete, and all the classrooms led off the corridors. I remember the playground at the back of the school being split and fenced to keep the girls and boys apart. During break times, the classes were split, and we took turns in using the quadrangle and the playing fields. I don't have many other memories of attending that school, as I hated it so much, I played truant whenever I could. I can't remember even one of the teachers' names, that's just how uninterested I was in the place.

Things must have been a lot more relaxed, as each time Jackie and I played truant, not once were we missed from class. We always attended the assembly and the first lesson, so we were in the register as attending.

But one thing stuck in my mind. On one occasion, my mother was ill in hospital. We were all given a letter to take home to give to our mothers, but when the teacher gave me my letter, I remember asking, 'Who shall I give my letter to?' The teacher enquired where my mother was and when I told her she was in hospital and I didn't have a father, she went into a panic. The teachers then went into a meeting to discuss my circumstances, as they should have been made aware of them.

At least during the time, I spent at that school, I was not bullied.

My friend Jackie was a year younger than me, and in a lower class. We were friends from home, as she lived with her parents and two brothers further into the village. She was very grown up for her age, had well developed breasts, and was very vivacious and popular, whereas I was very quiet, shy, and reserved.

One day Jackie asked me to 'bunk off' school with her. I didn't need much persuading, as I hated school. So, on the days that the children from several classes were walked across town to the tennis courts, we always ensured we were at the back of the line, then at one corner we hung back and did a runner. Not sure at first what we had planned to do or how we were going to get home, we seemed to just wander about the town. When we were making our way to the bus depot, an older man approached us and asked why we were not in school. We no doubt made up some story and told him that we wanted to get home but had no money for the bus. He gave us some money, so off we went and got the bus home.

Each time we played truant from school, we noticed that this man was always hanging around in the streets. We had to pass him to get to our bus stop, and eventually he started stopping us and chatting. I can't remember now what we chatted about, but he seemed more interested in Jackie, who was a lot more talkative than me.

One day, he told us that he had a television in his garage, and if we wanted, we could go with him and watch the TV. He was very persuasive, and as we had nothing else to do, we went with him.

The garage was quite a large building, which seemed to be on some waste ground in between some rows of houses. Inside it smelt of oil and petrol, was quite dark and gloomy, with not many windows. He had a couple of vehicles stored in there and lots of vehicle spare parts lying around. He said he liked tinkering with cars. He switched on the TV for us.

Looking around, I noticed there were some steps going up to a loft area above the garage, and I began to wonder what was up there. Surely, he didn't live there? After some time, which he had spent chatting with Jackie, he took her upstairs with him. I noticed he turned up the volume on the TV and told me to sit and watch it. I don't remember being that bothered about being left downstairs watching the TV, as we didn't have one at home, so I guess it was a bit of a novelty to me. I never knew what he and Jackie did together when they were upstairs; we never spoke about it, which looking back was odd really, as we were close friends. We used to talk about everything else.

On one occasion, the man took me upstairs, and I didn't like what followed. He sat me on his knee, started kissing me and touching me. It felt like he had me under a spell. I didn't want to do anything with him, but I was too scared and naïve to know how to get myself out of that situation. When I think about him now, I can still smell his breath on my face and feel his lips slobbering all over me. Looking back as an adult, I just thank goodness for certain times in the month, as I think he would have gone further than just touching. I can still get cross with myself even after all these years for letting myself down so badly. I felt this was my fault. This affects lives, so don't let it happen to you. Thankfully, children nowadays seem a lot more streetwise than when I was young.

That year couldn't end fast enough for me, to get away from school.

My mother had several part-time cleaning jobs, and as I got older and was well behaved, she would take me with her during the school holidays. The people she worked for didn't mind. I went to Mrs Harrison's house while Mum cleaned, and I don't recall what I actually did, but I imagine I would have had a book to occupy me. Mrs Harrison liked me; after all, she had nursed me back to health when I was a baby.

My mother also cleaned for the family next door, the Lewisham's, as she had been highly recommended to them by Mrs Harrison. I am not sure whether I ever went there. All I can recall is my mother telling me that if Mr Lewisham was at home when she finished work, he would drive her home in his sports car, which he drove very fast. That frightened my mother.

Just reminiscing here, I don't know what it was about my mother, but lots of things scared her. I remember we went to Knowsley Safari Park, and while driving through the animal enclosures, I stopped for a bit in the lions' area. My mother panicked, as she could see the young cubs watching our car wheels slowly moving. Even television programmes or films, like *Jurassic Park,* or any history programmes about dinosaurs, she wouldn't watch them and made us turn off the tv, to my and my stepdad's dismay. My stepdad enjoyed watching wildlife programmes, but as soon as any killing happened, off went the TV. She controlled our television, and she didn't even have a remote in those days.

Both these houses Mum cleaned were very nice and reflected the wealth of the owners. Mrs Harrison's had very high ceilings, with ornate cornices around, lush carpets on the floors, and a lovely bathroom – the first time I had seen one of those. It was so far removed from the house I lived in. Mrs Harrison would always give me something nice to eat when my mother had her break. Dr and Mrs Harrison had grown-up children: Alistair, who was training to be a doctor, and was in Scotland; and they had a daughter Harriet, who lived locally. My mother cleaned for her for a while.

Another house my mother cleaned was a strange one in some ways, so different to any of the others. My mother was only allowed in some rooms, while others were out of bounds. The rooms that she could access were very cluttered and the front room was packed with brass ornaments. Sitting in the fireplace was a huge brass Buddha, and before Mum left, she always rubbed his tummy and made a wish. My mother used to say that she always felt like someone was watching her. She didn't stay long in that job.

Of all the jobs I went into with Mum, my favourite by a long way was Kaye and Foley Photographers in the town. While mum was busy cleaning, I spent my time in the dark room with a Miss Lightburn, whose job was developing all the prints that had been taken by the photographers. I found this so enjoyable. The photos in those days were all sepia, and Miss Lightburn coloured them as needed by hand with watercolour paints, like an artist really. She could also disguise things, such as, if a bride looked like she had a pole coming out of her head, Miss Lightburn could disguise this with her paints. So never say a photograph never lies; some do! During my time spent with her, she taught me how to colour photos and would let me take some old pictures and paints home. I thoroughly enjoyed my time there.

During the longer summer school holidays, I went to work for a firm called Mahoods, who hired people to plant small tree saplings in fields in the village. I did this for the full six weeks, to the dismay of some of the older regular planters, as I was paid the same hourly rate as the adults who thought I couldn't keep up and plant as many as them. But I proved them wrong. I did just as much as them, and I had youth on my side and determination. Whatever I set my mind to, I will always give it my best shot.

CHAPTER 3

GROWING UP

There wasn't a lot to do for a young teenage girl living a semi-isolated life. My mother didn't like me having too many friends, as she was worried that they or their parents would be questioning me about who my father was, but she did allow me a few friends from the village.

The owner of the cottage we now lived in – our landlord – lived next door with his brother, who had some kind of mental condition. He never went out to work, but he did look after all the poultry they had. Each large hen cabin had a flock of hens and one cockerel. The cabins were cleaned out every day, and I spent many hours with him helping him to clean them out. The cockerels were not necessarily friendly but would tolerate us being around them. I remember one beautiful multi-coloured one who would strut his stuff, trying to impress all his lady hens, his feathers shining in the sun. He was a pleasure to watch. However, there was a white one we named Alfonso, who was vicious. He was going to protect his ladies and didn't take kindly to us in his territory, so he would fly at us if we got too close, claws extended.

When I was with Dave helping him with the hens, he talked a lot, but not about anything that made sense to me. When he wasn't actually doing any work, he spent his time staring up into the sky. He was always seeing things and kept talking about the 'train' that he could see travelling across the sky. I didn't know what he was referring to, as I couldn't see anything. The moon and stars fascinated him. Maybe he was seeing into the future. Having said that, on one occasion way before I had met Dave, I saw something in the sky while I was playing out, and when I told my mother, she said it would be an airship. Maybe those are what Dave was seeing. Who knows!

A black and white collie dog from a neighbouring farm was always hanging around, but I assume he came after the hens. One day it pinned me to the wall and bit my leg. My Aunt Hilda came to my rescue with her bottle of iodine and dressed the wound.

Another dog we had problems with was a large Airedale, from another farm further down the road. We had to cycle past this farm each time we went to town, and it was always stood by the gate then chase us when we went past. Maybe that's why I don't really like dogs that much; well, anyone else's, that is. I have loved dogs we have owned.

One teatime I was going home from work. I had left my bicycle at a garage where they let us park them when we went for the bus to town. I got off the bus and picked up my bicycle then started to ride home. It was a filthy night, a storm, with very strong winds and torrential rain. I had pulled my snood down over my eyes to keep out the rain, when suddenly I ran smack bang into the back of a parked car, buckling the front wheel of my bike. I ended up having to walk the rest of the way home. The New Causeway, as it was called, was a treacherous road, long and straight, and cars would speed along as though on a racetrack. The road was a lot higher than the surrounding fields on both sides, and there were deep ditches at the edges on both sides. It was always windy on that road. The eldest son of my friends from a neighbouring farm was cycling to our house one bonfire night in the dark, and sadly was hit by a speeding car. He died.

The cottage was rather crowded, especially when my mother started seeing a gentleman, Richard. Eventually they married, so then we had to move out. We were lucky and managed to get a council house in another village. So, we moved into that on my 17th birthday.

This property was a good step up, compared to the earlier ones I had lived in. It had all mod-cons, bathroom, two flushing toilets. On the ground floor was a lounge, which was a good size; it had two good windows to front and rear, so was a light airy room, and we had a coal fire. The kitchen was smallish, but had a good range of cupboards, a washing machine, and a cooker, hot and cold running water. The bathroom was small, but okay to accommodate a bath, hand basin, and toilet. But upstairs was best for me – three bedrooms, so I had my own room again, no sleeping with my mother or Aunt Hilda. (While still at the cottage, when mother married Richard, I had to move in to sleep with Aunt Hilda.)

The back garden was huge, but Richard had always been a keen gardener, so he grew all our vegetables and some flowers from seed. He had a decent-sized greenhouse which he heated in the winter. His favourite flower was the large-headed chrysanthemum, which is now my favourite. During late autumn he had a greenhouse full of them, just for his pleasure, and he treated them like babies. Richard worked for the council in various roles during his working life, after coming out of the Army during WW2. He was a very quiet, patient man, with a funny sense of humour. I never heard him swear once, and you couldn't pick an argument with him. He liked to have a dog around the house and he picked our Judy from a litter; he wouldn't have any of the other pups. She turned out to be a brilliant dog, my best friend, and confidant.

My mother did not invite me to their wedding, as she wouldn't allow me to take a day off work. Our relationship had never been that good, but I think that was the point that made it irrecoverable. From then on, we lived together under the same roof more as strangers than family. She never was a talker, and if you went to her with any problems, her answer was always the same, 'I don't know.' I could never walk about the house in my nightwear, because I was living with a man I didn't really know and I felt embarrassed for him to see me not fully dressed. So, it certainly wasn't a relaxed, happy household.

In the early 80s, the government allowed council house tenants to buy their house if they wished, so my stepfather bought ours in 1980 for just a few thousand pounds. I moved out in 1982 and moved into a bedsit, mainly to see if I could cope living on my own, before taking the plunge and buying my own home. I loved the freedom, so in 1985 I bought my own house. I remember being so thrilled that I threw myself on the floor in one of the bedrooms and rolled around. I was away from my mother now; I could live my own life.

As a youngster I had always wanted to learn to ride horses, but my mother said she couldn't afford the money it cost for one hour's lesson. When I got my first job as a shop assistant at Silverton's, on Tuesday afternoons the shop closed so I booked riding lessons.

My teenage years were relatively happy ones. I worked full-time and went out at weekends with friends or my boyfriend, either to the pictures or just around the town in the summer months. When I was old enough, we would pop into some country pubs for a pint. Our favourite pub at the time was The Brook; yes, it was built at the side of a babbling brook. It was a small country pub with cosy rooms and coal fires, and the landlord and staff were lovely. On the way home we stopped at The Bull for a tray of chips, sausage, and gravy. Sometimes Simon would just drive us straight home, and I have to say I was disappointed as I always looked forward to my supper.

I fancied getting a bit more mobile, so decided I would like to buy a Raleigh Moped. We found one for £25, so my mother lent me the money and I was given a payment card to pay her back so much a week, probably something like five shillings. This type of transport was not for me.

I was 19 when I started driving lessons with a local driving school. During my lessons, my instructor would direct me to a particular road, where I had to park up while he went into one of the houses. He wouldn't be very long, then we carried on with my lesson. I still got my full hour. My stepfather said it was probably his fancy woman he went to see.

When I took my test the first time, I was so nervous and I think that was the reason I failed. So, on the second attempt, my instructor suggested I bought something from the chemist to calm my nerves, He gave me the name of what I should buy (I have forgotten it now) and I sailed through that test, though I did feel a bit spaced-out. When I got back to work and told everybody I had passed, they couldn't understand why I wasn't jumping up and down, but I was just not with it. Imagine if that happened these days.

The first car I bought was a black Morris Minor 1000, which I paid £40 for from a guy in town who had been caught by the Police for driving the wrong way round a roundabout. He lost his licence, so decided to sell the car. It was a rust bucket, and I have no idea how on earth it kept going, but I got two years out of it (this was before MOTs!). It helped me gain my confidence on the road, though.

One car I had was a black Fiesta XR2, which I always felt good driving. I would wash and polish it every week until the bodywork shone. One night, I had gone to Fleetwood to a dancing school, and as I was driving home on the Blackpool Road, some lads drove along the side of me. Thinking they were trying to push me off the road, I slammed my foot down to the floor and, fortunately, my faithful little XR2 outran them, but it was a scary experience. Sadly, sometime later it was broken into and stolen from an NCP car park. When it was recovered by the Police, the thieves had smashed their way in through the boot and hammered the steering column to get it started. I had it repaired, but it never felt the same again

When I started having problems with my eyes, my hospital consultant advised me not to drive, ever since it has been taxis and buses for me.

For a number of years one of my interests was entering competitions. I subscribed to The Compers News, which was a good magazine and listed all the current competitions each month, sometimes even giving the answers. But I didn't have much luck. I seemed to be luckier entering competitions in local newspapers or on local radio shows. Three memorable prizes stick in my mind.

On the 3rd May, 1993, I entered a phone-in competition at one of our local radio stations, Red Rose Gold, based in Preston. I was lucky to get picked and the presenter on the night was Scottie McClue. When I got through, his guest for the evening was an astrologer, Peter Woods, who gave me an interesting reading. Amongst other things, he told me that I would never marry, because one man could never satisfy me. Noooo! not like that, cheeky! He referred to my varied, obscure interests, hobbies, and lifestyle, and said that I would need more than one person to share them with.

In another phone-in competition with the same radio station, the prize was a marble and wooden fire surround. I sent my name and phone number in, and again, I was lucky to get picked. When the phone went, you hadn't to say 'Hello', or you would be eliminated. What you had to say was, 'Win a fireplace from Living Fireplaces, Accrington.' I won, and I still have it in my lounge now.

The best competition I won was with the *Lancashire Evening Post* newspaper, when the prize was a helicopter ride around Blackpool. I loved that, as it was the first time I had been up in any type of aircraft. Even though all the front of the 'copter was glass' and sometimes you felt like you were going to fall forward, I still loved it; circling Blackpool Tower was something else. I wouldn't hesitate to go up in one again.

For years I was a great fan of the Spinners folk group. I went to many of their concerts, locally, or I would drive or sometimes a coach would be organised. I joined their official fan club, which met once a month in a room over a pub in Paradise Street in the city. They were great nights, because you had the group up close, and they would mingle and chat with you. Good times. Pete Goodall, who I was to meet later in life, also attended some of these nights. I was in the audience at one of their televised concerts and I just got home in time to watch it on the television. There I was, my full face on the screen, singing (miming, actually) my heart out. Well, no-one wants to hear me sing out of tune. It was a sad day when the group split up.

Talking of sad days, a theatre not far from my home was threatened with closure. It was one I had not been in, so I decided one day I would go and take a look around it. On arrival, it was heaving with school pupils, all in their uniforms and from a number of different schools. I just followed the crowd inside and started wandering about, trying to get my bearings. Eventually I found myself in a long corridor with many doors along each side. I carried on walking and reached the door at the bottom of the corridor, opened it, and walked through, only to find myself on the stage in the middle of a performance. I quietly retreated the way I had gone and eventually found my way out. At no point were there any security staff. The theatre did eventually close.

I do like having some kind of project on the go. I have a 'thinking' mind and hate to be idle. During 2005 I set up a scheme called 'Don't Just Sit There', with the aim of getting people off their bums and exercising. Prior to this, I had been attending a gym regularly and found how exercise could help me feel much better, fitter, and stronger. I wanted to help others do the same.

I set about approaching local sporting organisations for free taster sessions at their premises and was thrilled at the response I got. With the help of two local leisure centres and various clubs and groups, I was able to offer hourly sessions in the gym, dancing, archery, paint balling, martial arts, walking, cycling, golf, and hypnotherapy. I also got a nutritionist on board to give advice on diet. I then approached our local newspaper about it, and they printed an excellent article for me, called 'Get Moving for Mrs Motivator'. At the time there was a programme on TV called 'Celebrity Fit Club', so I approached them and told them what I was doing. They sent me a bag of goodies to give out to people. Someone from Radio Lancashire saw the article and invited me to chat about it on the radio.

I joined our local Home Watch group, firstly as a volunteer – mainly delivering leaflets round different areas. I was invited to join the committee after a while, which I did, but I had to push myself a bit as I am not used to doing things like this, which are well out of my comfort zone. After a while the secretary left, so our chairperson was looking for someone else to fill this role. I was approached and asked if I would do it and hesitantly agreed, as again it was out of my comfort zone. I found taking all the minutes a bit hard as I don't do shorthand, but I struggled through. However, I never really felt comfortable in the role, so I didn't stick it for long. I had retired by that time and felt that, having left work behind me and all the stress that it had involved, I didn't want to start putting myself into stressful situations when I didn't need to.

From around the early 70s, I joined a local walking club. I really do enjoy walking, and it was good to get away and see some lovely scenery in other counties. A coach trip was organized once a month and we went to various other counties to walk. Sometimes the coach dropped us off at a particular place and would wait for us if we were doing a round trip, or if we had a starting point and walking to another finishing point, the coach would wait at the finish for us. On the original walks, they did three levels – low, medium, and high – so you could choose how strenuous a walk you wanted to do. I did invest in some really good waterproofs and walking boots, as you need to be fully prepared when you are walking up hills and down dales. A lot of Kendal Mint cake was consumed on those walks by many of the members. We took refreshments with us, but on the way home we would stop at a pub and have a meal. These were thoroughly enjoyable trips out for me, until a couple of the youngsters got elected to organise and arrange the walks. They started to include a bit of climbing, rather than just walking, and that became a bit hard for me, so I eventually stopped going.

With Great Aunt Harriet collecting me to go off to work in the fields. I was about 18 months old. Can just see Lassie in the background.

Outside the farmhouse, the chapel in the background.

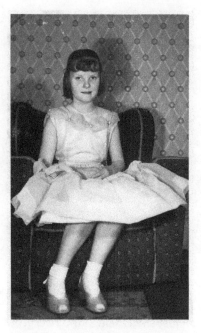

All dressed up, ready for the school party.

One Christmas with my mother, Great Uncle Ivor and
Great Aunt Harriet.

My mother, Florence.

Riding Tangerine (Tangy) on the beach in the 1960's.

New Quay Harbour, the fishing boat in the
foreground I took a fishing trip on.

Judy, my best friend and confidant, 1970's

At a local riding school in 1977. That is the indoor
school behind us. An hour later I had broken that
lower section of the wooden side of the school,
after Libra spooked and tossed me off through it.

Receiving my bronze medal for Latin at Dancers
in Preston. From Robert and Barbara Lichfield,
who were All England Champions in 1990.

My first attempt at scuba diving whilst on holiday in Greece.

I am a poor swimmer, so the instructor guided me.

CHAPTER 4

MY WORKING LIFE

I left school on a Friday, and on the Saturday my mother marched me into town. We went into some of the shops where she asked if they had any vacancies, and we did this until we found someone to give me a job. I started the following Monday. My mother wanted me earning.

My first job interview was with the manager of Silverton's shoe shop in the town. I went along for an interview, and the manager took me on for a trial period, as was the norm those days. He was a little concerned that I didn't want a short break or a holiday before starting work, but my mother would never have allowed that. And anyway, what was a holiday? My family had never had one of those! I was kitted out with a uniform – a navy nylon overall with a white collar, which I was to discover was very unpleasant to wear in the hot weather.

I enjoyed working there. The other staff members were nice and some of them became friends, who I went out socializing with. I met my first boyfriend there, as he worked in the men's department. I went out with him for several years but, deary me, my mother was not impressed at all. I remember a time when I was seeing another lad who used to cycle all the way to our house, and one day my mother got to the door before me and sent him away. I never saw him again.

The area manager would come to our shop periodically to do training sessions on how to sell shoes. He would tell us that if a lady came into the shop for a brown pair of shoes and we didn't have her size, rather than just apologising that we didn't have her size, we should bring out another colour for her to try on. Once she had it on her foot, if it fit and was comfortable, nine times out of ten she would buy the shoes. Some silly things do stick in your mind.

I stayed there for four years in my role as shop assistant, and I worked in the ladies and gents shoe department, as well as on the repair counter, which in those days was busy. People tended to have their shoes repaired, and stiletto heels were always losing the studs.

I earned £3.17.6d a week, which I got on a Friday in a wage packet. I had to hand over £2 to my mother towards my keep, and the rest was plenty to last me a week – bus fares, popping into Woolworths for snacks, and going out socially. My mother's best friend was a conductor on the buses, so when she was on my bus, I got a free ticket. It was only 2d.

Later, I was to find out that the manager of the shop had not been taking out any NI contributions, so when I changed jobs, I had to top this up.

During these four years, all the shops in our town closed on a Tuesday afternoon, so that's when I booked lessons at a local riding school. I took my first riding lessons on the beach, and there really wasn't much instruction, just basically being taught how to stay in the saddle through a trot and canter. My mother was so disapproving that I was spending – or should I say wasting – money just to have a ride on a horse. That's how she viewed it.

My mother's friend eventually got fed up working on the buses – too much hassle, she used to say – and started to look for another job. A new warehouse distribution centre was opening just a few miles from where I was living at the time, The Publishers Warehouse, and they advertised in our local paper for people to apply for the jobs. Frances got an application form but, after giving it a lot of thought, she chickened out and didn't apply. She gave the form to me and I sent in my application, had an interview, and got a job. This was in the late 1960's.

I had no experience in office work, so I was put in the filing department where I spent all my time just filing papers. It was a mundane activity, but the pay was good compared to what I had been used to. We did have an old mechanical version of an Index File Sorter, which made filing easier and quicker. I was situated in the typing pool. The room was quite large, and all around three walls were large filing racks, with windows on the outside wall. In the middle of the room sat all the typists and secretaries. After a while I became interested in typing, so I enrolled with Willy Scheidegger Touch Typing School, and more or less taught myself to type. Willy Scheidegger booked a room in one of our hotels in the town, and we went there for a few lessons. They loaned us the typewriter, but most of the contact with them was done by post. I learned to type well enough to get me a job in another department.

The Dispatch Office sent containers full of books to Third World countries on a regular basis. Mr Roberts, the Dispatch Manager, was a brilliant man to work for. Our office was tucked away at the back of the building on the ground floor. On one occasion I was looking for a new car. Mr Roberts had got the local newspaper on his way to work, as he did every week and he looked at the cars for sale. If he saw anything he thought may be suitable for me (he was like a father figure), he told me to sneak out and go and take a look before anyone else had the chance to buy it. I stayed in the Dispatch department for a few years. One challenge I faced was booking container space for the shipments. Maths has always been, and still is, a mystery to me, but the ladies at the end of the phone at the shipping terminals were very helpful. I really loved working for Mr Roberts, and shortly before I moved out, another lady joined us in the office, Carol, who became a lifelong friend of mine. When Mr Roberts retired, instead of replacing him, our company moved the Dispatch Department out into the warehouse. But hey, all good things have to come to an end.

There was a very large warehouse area containing stacks upon stacks of shelving, all holding books of various categories, all of educational value, plus some children's books. Any damaged books we could have, so I gained quite a collection of horse/vet and other medical books.

I left the Dispatch Department, along with Carol, and moved into the Order Processing office on the ground floor. We distributed books for many publishers, mostly educational and medical books, to schools and bookshops.

I was put in the invoicing section at first, checking that all the information on the invoices was correct before sending to the warehouse for dispatch. Our CEO was a Mr Smith, who was ex-military, and I used to muse seeing him walking around that he always looked like he was marching. He would come into the office one day a week and had us all shivering in our shoes, as he would randomly stop by a desk or two and ask us what we were doing. You had to know your job and be on top of things so that you could answer him clearly and precisely, explaining exactly what you were doing that day.

After a while I moved onto the VDU section, where I could use my typing skills again. We keyed in all the book orders by entering the bookseller's account number and the book ISBN numbers. After a while you got to know the bigger sellers' accounts off by heart, as we did the most popular book ISBNs, and it helped not having to look them up all the time. The information we entered into the VDUs was recorded on small tape cassettes. At the end of each day, the data from each cassette was copied onto a large magnetic tape which was then transmitted down to Head Office down south, then overnight they processed the data and produced the invoices that we received the following day.

I must have shown an aptitude for computer work, as I was to be trained in the processing of these cassettes and the evening transmission. This meant working longer hours, as the transmitting all depended on whether the dial-up line was strong enough to allow us to send all the data. Sometimes it failed, and we would have to start the run again.

The building we occupied was quite a rambling place, with many of the rooms still quite derelict. Sometimes during my lunch hour, I would go exploring the rooms on the upper floors we didn't use. I remember opening one door and it was a good job I didn't step forward, as it was just a door to the outside. I could have fallen to my death. No health and safety in those days! I shouldn't have been there, but I love exploring.

Over the 20 plus years I worked there, the company names changed many times and publishers came and went, until we were left with just one. Greenall's Publishing took over and became the sole publisher we worked for. This meant that a lot of staff, I believe 75 percent, were made redundant. This meant the building we were in was far too large, so I believe a deal was done with another company a few miles away and we swapped premises to move into a smaller building.

The new premises were just around the corner from where I lived; really handy. It seemed strange that every department was now on such a smaller scale, though. I was in the computer room as a computer operator, with only two lads and a manager. Our roles were to process all the inputted orders and produce monthly reports for our director. As our manager was not always in the office, it was decided to create a supervisor role. All three of us had to apply and we were interviewed, but I was lucky enough to get the job. I suddenly found myself in charge of the other two lads, who were really super and we had always worked well as a team. I was also in charge of the whole computer room when the boss was out of the office.

The manager of our computer department started to get itchy feet and felt he had skills for a larger organisation, so he eventually left to go and work in a big city. Before he went, discussions took place between him and our director and it was decided not to replace him, but to promote me. I was given the title of Computer Operations Manager. I was thrilled but nervous at the same time, as this took me well out of my comfort zone. I now had to deal with suppliers, maintenance engineers, and other heads of departments. Unfortunately, my mother could not even say how proud she was of me becoming a manager, despite the fact that no-one in our family had ever been a manager of anything.

The computer room that I was now in charge of was nothing like the computers of today. We had four large disk drives, one fixed and three removable. The removable ones looked like a pile of LP records stacked one on top of the other and were very sensitive to temperature. In fact, they were sensitive to anything, and we backed them up daily onto large magnetic tape.

The following summer, the computer system was upgraded from a Systime 5000E, which was based on a Dec 11/34 processor, to the PDP 11/84. The operating system was RSX (RSX being the trade name of the Digital Equipment Company). All the software programs were written in the language Vista, as this software was quite simple and straightforward to write simple programs. We did have a full-time programmer, but I had a dabble and wrote a couple of simple programs myself. At the time we didn't use the more common languages of Cobol, Basic, or C. The processor had 2 megabytes (2024k) memory, mostly taken up by the operating system. The system supported 16 working VDUs locally and 2 VDUs remotely in our head office. We had a few storage cabinets housing one RA81 fixed Winchester Disk, with storage capacity up to 456megabytes. This disk is a sealed unit, therefore cannot be removed from the cabinet. Also, in this unit was a TU80 magnetic tape drive which ran at 1600 BPI (bits per inch). We used 2400ft (40megabyte) and 3600ft (60megabyte) tapes throughout the day, backing up data. We had three storage modules or the DEC equivalent RM05 removeable disk drives. They each had a storage capacity of 256megabytes. As these disks can be removed from the drives, they required periodic cleaning and inspection. They also had a habit of crashing. Even a speck of dust would make one crash. On one occasion when we had a crash, I removed the disk from the drive and out strode a spider. When the engineer arrived to repair it, he couldn't believe how a spider had even got into the drive. The remote VDUs and a character printer in the Head office were connected into our system via a direct line, using a modem and an 8-line statistical multiplexer, with a maximum speed 9600 band BPS (bits per second). The printer speed was 2400 BPS (or 200 characters per second).

Some of the larger bookshops used a teleordering system. They entered all their orders from customers into a terminal, then at the end of the day this file was transmitted over to IBC – a computer run by Software Sciences. They collated all the orders for various publishers, and for the ones we dealt with, they sent the orders over to us via a modem and protocol converter, which converts the data into a format our computer software could understand. This is a brilliant way of ordering, as it cuts out all the paper postal orders and is much faster.

The computer room was airconditioned to control the temperature, with the air circulated, cooled, filtered, and humidified as it passed through the unit. The temperature was a constant 72 degrees and the humidity quite high to stop static electricity building up around the drives, so it was lovely to work in during the hot summer months. When the computer room doors were locked, that automatically activated the fire protection system and we had smoke detectors in the ceiling. In the event of a fire, a bell would ring, and all staff had 30 seconds to vacate the room, then a siren sounded then the halon gas would be released. The gas cylinders were housed two in the ceiling and one under the floor, so the gas then circulated around the installation, snuffing out the fire without causing any damage to the equipment, as it was a non-corrosive substance. Thankfully we never had a fire.

In addition to all the processing work from booksellers and publishers, we also ran an Artists Book Club, royalties for authors, Local Educational Councils (LEA), and the Journal Advertising Ledgers.

All the operators' VDUs in the office were linked into the system, with all the cables running under the false floor of the computer room. I grew confident at setting up new users as and when necessary, and I became well respected at being capable of keeping all VDUs running at their optimum. If problems did occur and I couldn't fix them, I would have an engineer on site within four to eight hours. That was proven when I left, and a friend and colleague told me how I was missed, because there was no longer anyone on site to sort out the problems. That meant a lot.

Our ultimate role in the computer room was to produce the monthly reports for our director. We would shut off all input on the last Friday of a month, start the processing programs running Friday night, then we would go into the office

Saturday and Sunday to print everything off, as we had to have the report on the director's desk when he came in on the Monday. My two lads along with me did this on a rota, which worked very well.

It could sometimes be a bit scary working in the building on your own at night. Above our offices was a corrugated tin roof, which didn't half rattle when it was windy. Legend has it that the place was haunted, and the story goes that a man hanged himself in the warehouse many years ago. I have tried researching this to find out who he was. One night I was working alone in my office. The kitchen was on the far side of the warehouse, so to make a drink I had to walk in the dark right across the warehouse. That particular evening, when I went to the kitchen, I felt a strong presence that someone was watching me, and I couldn't wait to get back to my office. Later that same evening, I was sitting at my desk when the room started to feel like it was closing in on me. I felt a presence again, and it grew so strong that I grabbed my bag, locked the door, ran out of the building and went home. I went back the following day to finish off the work.

On another occasion when it was Michael on the rota, I was at home and the phone went. It was Michael all he said was, 'will you come and take me home please?' He lived literally around the corner. I knew what had happened, so I jumped in the car and whipped round to work. When I arrived, he was standing at the front door as white as a sheet, but he wouldn't tell me what had happened.

When it was Stephen's turn on the rota, he had a dog which he always took in with him. It puzzled me why at the time, but now thinking back, it could have been for protection.

On another occasion, when the girls were arriving for work at 8am, Gladys walked into the office and saw a man in a dark suit, wearing a black bowler hat, walk into the lady's toilets. She hurried in after him to tell him he had gone into the wrong toilets, but there was no-one there.

During my time working for Greenall's, they celebrated their centenary in business. To mark the occasion, they held a special event and invited many people – authors, publishers, local councillors, and other local dignitaries – from around the area. All the heads of departments were instructed to give a tour of our own areas and I was asked to give a talk and presentation of what happened in our computer room. I was totally out of my comfort zone with this and had to call on my old boss for some pointers. He helped me put together a package and presentation, but by all accounts, I carried it off brilliantly. I was praised for my presentation and knowledge of what I did, and I even got an offer of a job from the owner of a well-known book shop in London.

For the presentation I wore my best bib and tucker. I also wore a pair of high stiletto heel shoes to try and make myself look a bit taller. After the presentation one of my colleagues told me that he had been watching me walking about the room, now and again standing on the air-conditioning grills in the floor and was worried that one of my heels was going to get stuck. Thankfully, it didn't, as that would have really put me off my stride.

Greenall's was a good firm to work for, as they looked after their employees. All managers were in BUPA. Annually, the bosses organised a cricket match, when the reps, managers, and anyone who liked or could play cricket could join in. They put on a coach and accommodation down south where their head office was. I went one year, but I have to say that sitting all day watching cricket is not for me. It's as bad as watching paint dry. But I was just trying to be sociable. They were also very good if you had any health issues, an operation, or an accident, and you could take advantage of places to go and convalesce, all paid for by the company. If they had a good year and the reps had hit their monthly targets, we got a healthy bonus, sometimes also a bottle of plonk.

Just before I left, our CEO bought a PC word processor for his secretary to replace her typewriter. When it was brought into the office, all the girls went and stood around it, gazing at it, wondering what it did. This was the start of modern technology.

Eventually the company had yet another buyout and another name; we were now called Latimer's and the Head Office was in Croydon. They quickly decided to move all the processing systems down to Croydon, which meant I was to be made redundant, as it wasn't possible to slot me back into an operator's role. I told my mother what had happened and received a typical reply from her: 'Pfft, look, no-one wants you.' She was always ready to mock me at every opportunity.

I left the company in the early nineties with a decent pay-out, but foolishly decided to take some time out before looking for another job. I totally enjoyed my freedom for the following nine months then started looking for employment. But I discovered, talking to staff in the Jobcentre, that if a person is out of work for more than six months, they are deemed as almost unemployable. All I was offered at the time was a place on an employment training scheme, which was based at our local hospital, so I thought I had better take that. With hindsight, it was a big mistake.

During the months I attended the scheme, Orchard Training, which was full-time, I gained a few qualifications which had been sadly lacking while I was at school. During those 12 months, we were sent on placements in various hospital departments. I threw myself totally into the work, unlike some of the others in the group, who just wasted their time. I spent some time working in Human Resources, which I enjoyed, and at the end of my stint there, the director asked me into his office, thanked me for all my help and told me that if there had been any vacancies, he would have offered me a job. I think we got paid £10 a month on that scheme.

Whilst on the course, a secretary in one of the other hospital sites, in the community, collapsed at the photocopier, so while she was in hospital, and for the interim period, Orchard Training was approached to see if any of their 'students' would be suitable to fill in. I was put forward straightaway, due to my maturity and clerical experience, and was sent over to the community offices for an informal chat with Mr Harrington, the manager. He took me on initially for three months, but this was extended to six months.

I was based in the absent secretary's office, and the lady in question was a long-time member of staff and very well liked. If I tried to move anything in her office, I was told off and told to put it back. Her nameplate disappeared off the door and I got scolded for that, even though it wasn't me. After a few months, sadly, the lady died, and for a while the atmosphere in the office was difficult, but understandable. I was offered the post on a permanent basis. Oh, how I wish I had turned it down.

I had a new computer software to familiarise myself with LocoScript, then we moved over to Word Perfect.

My role involved being a secretary to four departments: Finance, Child Protection, HIV and Sexual Health, and Voluntary Services. They were all very supportive of me.

The Finance Director was a kind man, so gentle, helpful, and patient, as I knew nothing about finance. The Child

Protection Manager wrote a manual about Child Protection and, of course, I had the job of typing it all up. She was including pictures and diagrams, which meant I had to leave space for her to put in her pictures. I was pleased with my efforts, and apparently at the presentation she was giving, many compliments were given for the manual. I had not done anything like that before. The three staff members who ran the HIV and Sexual Health Team were really nice – one lady and two men – and as their titles suggest, they were trying to eliminate sexually transmitted diseases amongst the community. I didn't enter their office very much and always had to knock before they unlocked the door. This was to stop clients from just wandering in. Once inside their office, on display was an enormous selection of condoms – all colours, flavours, sizes, types – and tables displaying any amount of sex toys, every type you can imagine. This opened my eyes somewhat. As it happened, we were all Queen fans, and on the day that Freddie Mercury died all four of us sat crying.

I also worked with the two ladies who ran the Voluntary Service, but I didn't really do much for them, just the odd letter. The lady who was in charge was always teasing me about boys, as I didn't have a boyfriend at the time. This was until...

I had been taking dancing lessons, but my dance teacher had an operation on his leg. He had a varicose vein removed, so his leg was in plaster. To get him out of the house, I went to pick him up and we went to a pub for a bite to eat. Who should come in but the two ladies from Voluntary Services. Now, my dance teacher was a young, tall, handsome chap, and as the ladies walked past us, I was given the 'look'. They thought he was my boyfriend, so I let them think that.

...I was never teased again.

I was moved into the Computer Room after a while, to join two part-time ladies, and soon settled in and really loved the job. The Director of Finance acted as our line manager. He was wonderful; we were just left to get on with the day-to-day running of the department. Our job involved collecting clinical data from all the community staff, e.g., District Nurses, Health Visitors, Podiatrists, Speech and Language Therapists, plus many others. Initially they filled in paper forms which we input into the computer system. After a while the paper forms were upgraded, and all the staff were issued with hand-held devices which they keyed all the information into. These were brought into our office by the end of each month for us to download the data onto the main computer. At the end of each month, we ran a suite of programs that processed the information and produced reports. From the reports, we recorded information to be sent off to the DOH (Department of Health), the purpose of which was to ensure we got a good budget from the Health Authority for the following year.

Eventually we got a new manager. On the first day in the job, we were called into her office for a talk, during which we were told that she 'had inherited us and we were not her choice of staff'. Then she sent us out with some written tests to complete. We were shocked, to say the least, and my colleagues both left soon after that – one retired, and the other found another job. If I'd had any sense, I would have followed them. But my stubborn side came out and I was determined to not let her push me out of the job I loved. For the following three months I was on my own in the department, and I was in my element organising and keeping everything ticking over. I never got behind, and all the reports were produced for the month end. Surprisingly, my manager left me alone. During this time, she advertised for another person to join our team, and eventually another lady came to work with me.

One of the other managers had noticed how hard I had worked during those months I was in the department alone and suggested I was promoted to Supervisor. I accepted this, as the pay working for the NHS was poor compared to what I had earned working for Greenall's. By that time, I had a mortgage, so this pay increase was welcome. But this did not go down well with my manager, who didn't approve of my promotion.

Even though I loved the job, it was difficult going into work each day when my manager was favouring my colleagues and being horrible to me. At one point I started having dark thoughts, wondering whether my life was worthwhile when all I had at the time was work; I had no social life to speak of. However, a manager from another department came to my rescue and removed our current manager to another area. What a relief that was for me! I will be eternally grateful to him. He doesn't know it, but he saved my life. Bullying can destroy lives.

When I bought my own house in the mid-eighties, my mother sulked with me for weeks, which I found quite funny. Why she could never be happy for me, I don't know. I remember on one occasion when I had booked a holiday, she commented, 'I never had a holiday, so why should you?'

It wasn't long before the NHS underwent yet another reorganisation and a name change. This major change meant many of us were moved to different locations, including me.

I started work in an administrative role which involved secretarial duties for my new manager and keeping the stationery cupboard well stocked, plus other general office duties. All other members of staff in this office were male except for the manager. I enjoyed working in that office in the early years, my male colleagues were a joy to be around, full of fun, things changed when new members of staff came into the department, the bullying started again. but after a while I was moved elsewhere into Human Resources.

What a repetitive job that was. Typing out contracts was a bit more interesting. But at least the other girls in the office were good to work with. There was a spell when I was the only one in the office; I think the others went off sick, and one might have been on holiday. I managed to keep all the general duties ticking along, but I couldn't deal with any policy or contract queries, as I wasn't trained or qualified for that. My role in Human Resources while on the Training Scheme was a lot more interesting.

During yet another office re-shuffle, I was moved again to a community clinic further away from home, which involved a horrendous daily journey each way. Instead of having a full-time job, they gave me two part-time ones, working across various clinics.

For the main job, I found myself working in an old building, in an office with one other staff member, who I did have a laugh with. Our sense of humour was the same, fortunately. I was working with School Nurses, and I would say that 80 percent of my day was spent filing. There was hardly any typing at all, just moving children's files from cabinet to cabinet. I went to one of the high schools with the nurse one day while she did her vaccinations, and I handed out the forms to the children. I have to say working with children is the last job I would have ever chosen; it wasn't for me. At least the School Nurses and Health Visitors were very good to me and a pleasure to work for.

To fill in my hours, I worked with the District Nurses. Now, I loved that job. I did most of their clerical work and some of their stats. They were a brilliant bunch of nurses, but I was only allowed to do a few months there. If I could have worked in that job full-time, I probably would have stayed till I reached full retirement age.

In the end, I worked half a day at the main clinic, then I was sent anywhere to cover for staff holidays or sickness. I stuck it for nine months, then decided to take early retirement.

One day, though, I had a bit of a chuckle. While working at one of the clinics, the lady I shared an office with had a mobile phone and she had a 'wolf whistle' as the sound for her text alert. One day we had a plumber come in to fix our heating radiator, and as he was bent over the radiator with his 'bum' facing me, my colleague's mobile went off (she was just out of the office at the time) and this shrill, loud wolf whistle rang out around the room. The plumber spun round and said sharply to me, 'Was that you?' 'No, I replied. He said, 'Well, there's only you and me here.' I don't think he was too pleased.

It's ironic really that I started my office working life as a filing clerk at the age of 19 and ended my working life as a filing clerk when I retired.

Looking back on my years in the NHS, they were the worst of my life. I suffered greatly at the hands of bullies for many years. If any of my readers are suffering, don't suffer like I did; do something about it. Tell someone; someone preferably in authority.

I have often wondered where I would have got a job if I had turned down the earlier offer to work in NHS. I do think I made a bad decision. But hey! I didn't have a crystal ball, plus I needed a job.

Being constantly bullied does have a profound effect on your life, and it drove me into isolation. I withdrew into myself. I put up huge barriers around me so that no-one could get close, and I didn't trust anyone. I still don't today. All I wanted was to fit in and be accepted as a member of the team. During my younger life I was neglected and abused, both emotionally and physically. So please, if this happens to you, tell someone.

Unfortunately, for people who find themselves being bullied, especially by their seniors, it always seems to come down to the thin line of 'clash of personalities' rather than anyone admitting to being a bully.

If I'd had a 'normal' life, with support, I know I could have made something of myself and forged a career. But being so timid and introverted and always being knocked back, stopped me from doing anything. I know you can't choose who your biological parents are, but if life is not working for you, dear reader, do something about it.

CHAPTER 5

OFF ON MY HOLIDAYS

Holidays, ah yes. Now that I am independent, I do treat myself now and again to a holiday – much to my mother's disapproval. She still thinks they are a waste of money and will always say, 'What have you got to show for them?' I can also remember hearing her say to me when I was off on one holiday, 'I never had that opportunity, so why should you?' She never supported me or encouraged me in anything.

As a school child, we alternated between our home and my Aunt Audrey's down south. One year I would go and stay with them for six weeks, and the next year they would come and stay with us. Although Aunt Audrey was always very good to me, these to me weren't real or proper holidays.

My first ever holiday away from home, I went to Newquay for a week on a Golden Rail Holiday in May 1975. It was a really good holiday; the rail company you booked with organized everything and you got reserved seats on all the trains. On departure, you handed your luggage to the conductor on the train, and the next time you saw it was when you got off the last train at your destination. I may have been on three or four trains during the whole journey. At the station of your destination, a coach was waiting for you to take you to your hotel. Included in these holidays were cheap tickets for train journeys.

I stayed in a small hotel, The Avondale, which was close to the seafront. The beauty of going in spring is that the hotels have redecorated or refurbished during the winter, so you get nice clean fresh rooms, and they are quiet. The Avondale Hotel was nice, and there was just one other lady on her own staying there. She was recovering from a major operation and her husband had sent her on holiday to recuperate. We became good friends and went out somewhere each day, including a trip to Land's End, leisurely walks around the many bays around Newquay, and looked around the local zoo. We also went to the Helston Floral Day, and it was lovely to see all the men and women dressed up, dancing down the streets and going in and out of all the houses which had all been trimmed up with flowers. We tended to go to shows in the evening or to see a film. On our last night, we went to see a Western type of film. Both of us were engrossed in the plot, when this cowboy came on screen, pointed a gun and shouted, 'Stick 'em up!' My friend next to me, flung her arms up in the air. A group of young lads were sat in the row behind us and they were howling and rolling about laughing.

The following year I went back to Newquay on Golden Rail Holidays again (May 1976). I stayed in a different hotel this time – a little larger one, and it had a bar. The hotel was nice, but a little further back from the beach. The only thing that got to me on that holiday was that a family arrived and one of the elderly ladies in the group was taken ill. It appeared she had brought a stomach bug with her, and the poor hotel owner was constantly mopping up. With my phobia of that sort of thing, I worried every day I stayed there whether I would catch it. Thankfully I didn't; nor did anyone else. Not a very relaxing holiday, though.

Going so early in the season can have its downside. For most of the week it was very foggy and there always seemed to be a heavy sea mist rolling in. But I enjoyed my time away from home and I did a few trips out, taking advantage of my discounted rail tickets to visit St Ives, Plymouth, Polperro, and Penzance. Even that early in the season, seaside stalls and shops were open and I enjoyed walking around some lovely sandy beaches. I booked to go on a fishing trip, hoping to see a shark (*Jaws*), though I was a bit wary when I saw how small the boat was. As we set off, it got a bit choppy and it didn't take long for land to disappear way into the distance. A young lad on the trip spent most of his time with his head over the side of the boat, so I made sure I was not down wind. All in all, it was a good holiday and I had another good journey home on the trains. Pity they stopped doing these holidays.

I decided to venture further afield, so in 1980 I booked my first holiday abroad. I booked with a singles' holiday firm called Buddies, which was a Package holiday suited to the age groups 18-30s. no-one checked your age at the time of booking, admin had booked a couple of pensioners on this holiday for the following week, on arrival they were not happy, and I had no idea that it was this travel firm's first year in operation.

I was booked on an evening flight from Manchester Airport to Rhodes – one of the Greek Islands. When we were up in the air I gazed from my window seat up at the moon in disappointment; I had expected it to look closer to us. The flight was fine, and it seemed no time at all before we were touching down in Rhodes. Flying over the island made it look so small and you could hardly see the runway. The plane felt like it was nose-diving down, but obviously it wasn't. When alighting from the aircraft, two things shocked me: all the men with guns surrounding the plane, who I assumed were soldiers; and the other thing was the heat. I had never experienced anything like that. I am not a fan of very hot weather, so began to wonder what I was doing there.

Two reps from Buddies – a young couple – met the arrivals and took us to the coach for drop-offs at various hotels. I had booked in a 3* hotel called The Edelweiss in Faliraki, very close to the beach. Once settled into my twin-bedded room, we were all free to explore Faliraki for the rest of the day. Evening meal was at a local restaurant, which is when we were all introduced to each other. I can't say I like Greek food, as everything seemed to have aubergine in it, but I did like the Ouzo.

The first full day of holiday started with a meeting with our reps. As they were from the UK, they understood what it is like for white Brits to suddenly find themselves in such heat. We were supplied with water throughout our stay and, to my surprise, we were given lots of watermelon to eat. They seemed very plentiful so maybe they are grown in Greece. Just as well I love watermelon. I found out later those watermelons help to protect you from the sun's UV rays, so they are handy to have around in a hot climate.

After a few days, a young girl was moved into my room to share. That's the only downside to travelling alone, you can end up sharing a room with a stranger. She seemed a quiet girl, but after a few days together, one morning both reps burst into our room, took all my belongings and my suitcase, emptied it on the bed and went through everything. Apparently, the girl had reported something of hers had gone missing. I didn't have it. From then on, when I went out on tours, I locked all my things in my case and took the key with me, so she couldn't plant anything on me.

I went on some of the daily excursions on offer, even though they were not included in the price. They weren't very expensive, and it was a good way to see the island. One trip I booked on was a journey through the orange groves by horse and carriage, but when I saw the condition of the animals, there is no way I was going to ask any of those horses to pull me in a carriage. They were all malnourished, full of sores, and some even lame. When I objected to joining the rest of them, I was told, 'It's their way of life and we can't inflict our standards on them.'

I went on a boat trip. It didn't go very far out to sea, but I got the chance of a scuba dive. As at that time I couldn't swim very well, the instructor took me down and kept hold of me, I enjoyed that, but the only problem was the goggles were a bit big and let in water. Apart from that it was very enjoyable. Some of the lads in our group weren't allowed on that trip, as they had been drinking heavily the night before, while some of the girls didn't fancy going underwater. I will have a go at most things.

On our excursions, the two reps always accompanied us, and a group of young women seemed to become obsessed with the male rep's 'package' when wearing shorts. I heard them muttering that it wasn't all 'him', so one day we were on the beach and one of girls ran up to him and pulled his shorts down. Poor guy, he must have been mortified as, yes, it was packing.

Everything was going along nicely, and I was having a very enjoyable holiday until the reps got us all together one day and informed us that some of our rooms had been double booked by admin. As a result, they were moving some of us out into private homes in the Greek countryside to spend the rest of our holiday staying with local families.

I was moved out, along with a couple of girls who had come together. They were very nice, two police officers from

London, and we got on quite well. A few of the lads were also moved out. My room was clean but very basic and the food was okay. As we were out during the day, it didn't matter really. But when it came to having a shower, it was in an outhouse and was just a hosepipe with a rose on the end. I kid you not! We were given a torch to take in with us. When I switched on the torch, the walls were covered with cockroaches or some other beetles, and there was nowhere to put your towel and spongebag. I think we all only went in there once.

Another trip I recall was a day out away from the coast. We travelled in jeeps, which are very bumpy vehicles to ride in over a long period of time, and we all got covered in sand. None of us went for a shower when we got back to the house. I think we all stayed dirty for the rest of the holiday.

When it came time to go home, I was lucky. Flying to Manchester, my seat on the plane was available, but for the people flying to London their seats had been double booked. So, they had to stay in Rhodes for a few more days.

I saw this as an adventure, and put it all down to experience, but I wonder what people today would have made of it. Compensation claims flying in from every direction, I would imagine.

It was another three years before I took another adventure. In September 1983, I took a trip to the USA to stay with a friend, Denise, in North Carolina. Denise, who is American, had lived in the USA with her husband Ray, but when her marriage ended in divorce, she made a fresh start by moving to the UK to live with her long-time pen pal, Stuart. She and I met when she got a job working in the same office as me. As our friendship developed, we went out socialising around our town. At the same time, her relationship with Stuart was getting stronger and they became romantically involved. Stuart was a lovely person, thoughtful and kind; I never knew Ray, so can't say what he was like. Eventually Denise and Stuart married, and they moved back to live in her hometown in the USA.

Denise got a job there with Piedmont Airlines, and Stuart started work for Denise's father John, who had a string of gasoline stations throughout North Carolina. He put Stuart to work running one of them, but as Stuart had no experience in the oil industry or running a station, unfortunately he didn't do very well. He eventually got a job in a cigarette factory, churning out cigarettes by the thousands. During my visit, Denise took me to Stuart's place of work to show me how their factories operate. What a noise! The machines were so deafening, and all the men working there had ear protectors on. I was amazed at just how many cigarettes they made.

Denise and Stuart had a very attractive property on the outskirts of North Carolina. To me, it looked like a small mansion house and stood in its own grounds. Neither of them liked gardening, so it was just down to lawn and a few trees, and they had a ride-on mower to cut all the grass. They had a little black, brown, and white spaniel Archie; it was such a lovely area to walk a dog. Denise told me that they get pestered a lot by Real Estate Agents when they have been in one property for a length of time. Always trying to get them to move. One thing impressed me, they were very conscious when driving not to go over the speed limit, if they got caught speeding, they didn't get points on their licence like we do back in the UK, but they got an increase on their insurance premiums, which could be quite hefty apparently.

Inside the house, which to me seemed an upside-down house, all the living rooms were upstairs to take advantage of the views, while the bedrooms were downstairs. In one of the lounges, they had quite a large picture of our Queen on one wall, which I was quite impressed with. The rooms were tastefully decorated in pastel colours, and the kitchen had every appliance and gadget you could think of. What fascinated me was the double sink, but it wasn't really. One of them was actually the waste disposal, but it was the first time I had seen one of those.

From the ground floor were steps to a lower floor, which was the entertainment room. It was kitted out with a bar, with many optics up on the wall, a few bar stools, a large TV, and all the gadgets that go along with it. There was also a snooker table, but I'm not sure who played snooker, as I never got the impression Stuart did. There weren't any TVs in any of the upstairs rooms, so they must have always gone down to the entertainment room to watch anything.

You had to go outside to access the garage, which was quite large. It housed the laundry area and, wow, her washing and drying machine were huge – more like industrial ones compared to ours back home. The air conditioning unit was in there, too. How wonderful was air conditioning? When you had spent the day outside in that heat, to go home and walk into a cool room was fabulous. The only downside to that for me was the constant noise it made, and if you sat by any of the vents in the lounge, you got a draught all the time.

It was a few minutes' drive to the nearest shopping mall to get groceries. One thing I did find difficult was getting up in the mornings, getting washed and dressed, then going out for breakfast. They didn't have any cereals or anything in the house for breakfast, as their normal everyday life consisted of get up, dressed, set out for work, go to a drive thru, pick up bacon sandwich or similar, then carry on to work. Not my thing, I'm afraid. But while I was there, I just accepted it. I was also introduced to Blue Cheese dressing, which I really liked.

A week after I arrived, Stuart's brother Cyril came over from the UK to join us. They took me out to a few wonderful places during my three weeks' stay.

Denise took me to meet some of her family who live in St. Augustine. A lovely place, totally different to North Carolina, it is a lot more rural, and I found the roads dusty. We all went to a roadside café for our meal, and it was just typical of the type of establishment we see on our TV screens of American roadside cafes. Some of the houses I saw along our journey had more colourful gardens, with climbing plants all around the doors, whereas the properties around where Denise lived tended to have gardens with just lawns and trees. They didn't seem to go in for flowering plants.

We went down to Florida for a few days. As Denise worked for an airline, she was entitled to discounts on hotels or rooms, so she booked us in a room close to Disneyworld. While she was in booking the room, Cyril and I had to stay out of sight. It was common practice there for rooms to be booked just for two, then the rest of the party would be smuggled in, and that is what we did. The room had two double beds, so I had to share with Denise while the two men shared the other. Rooms are booked but you don't get breakfast. So again, it was a case of going out and looking for somewhere to eat.

Disneyworld was something else. I was so mesmerized. All the rides we went on were out of this world. The shops and the stalls selling memorabilia were at every turn, and I bought a few T-shirts and other things to take home for a friend's small children. But on the journey home the airline lost my suitcase, and when it did eventually turn up at my door, some weeks after I had got home, the locks were broken. It had been opened and all my gifts and souvenirs were missing. I'm not sure that my friend believed me, but I was so disappointed.

However, I did have my photograph taken with Minnie Mouse.

We had a day at SeaWorld, and all I can really recall from that day was sitting and watching a poor orca swimming round and round in a smallish pool, doing tricks for us. I did have my photograph taken by the model of *Jaws* from the film, though.

On another trip out, Denise and Stuart took us to the Space Centre to see some of the rockets. I'm not sure if these were models or the real ones that had been out into space, but there was one in particular that looked like it could have been used. There were cases with models of astronauts in and all the paraphernalia they have to wear, which was more up Cyril's Street than mine.

Another memorable trip out was to meet Denise's parents, John and Cecilia. Wow! What a place they lived in. Now we are talking mansion proportions, but I suppose if you're in the oil industry you do have a dollar or two. Cecelia also had a good job; she was a cosmetic buyer for a very well-known American high street retail business.

The approach to their house was like driving through a park. Once parked up, you entered the property through a massive conservatory, which was full of huge trees, plants, vines, and a large pond with a waterfall.

Inside the house was just as impressive. There were very large rooms with high ceilings and tall windows with beautiful drapes. All the rooms I saw were beautifully decorated. I was offered a cup of tea, but while we were sitting drinking our beverage, their little dog wandered into the room. It was a little dachshund, who for some reason made a beeline for me and started humping my leg. All John could say was, oh, he likes you'. I was embarrassed; it wouldn't leave me alone. Even when Cecilia took me into her dressing room to show me all the cosmetics and perfumes she had, the dog kept clinging onto my leg. She had drawer upon drawer full. As she showed me all the different fragrances and lipsticks, she kept pushing various ones into my hands, saying, 'Here, have this.' I left with quite a few and I assume worth quite a bit of money.

Well, all good things must come to an end, and when it was time to go home Denise had booked my flight for me. Working in the industry, it was easier for her and she booked me a window seat on both flights. First, I had to take a small internal flight back to JFK, then my main flight home to the UK. Both journeys were good, smooth, and without any problems. On the way home, I seemed to be surrounded by a group of workers going back home to the UK. One was sitting next to me and at first, he tried to coax me to change seats so his mate could have mine. No way was I giving up my window seat to sit in the middle of the aircraft. Then when our food was brought round, he said to me, 'You don't want that, do you?' He was hungry and trying to cadge mine as well. However, I sat and enjoyed my meal, to his dismay. It was a very enjoyable holiday, apart from my suitcase being lost.

In 1990 I went to Tunisia with a friend from work. We flew from Manchester and stayed in the hotel Le Saphir in Hammamet. We had a ground floor room with French doors to the garden area, which was nice as we could enter and leave through this door. Only problem was that at night people were constantly walking past, so it was difficult to get to sleep. It wasn't very clean, either; the bedding was okay, but the carpet looked like it had not seen a vacuum cleaner for some time.

As the hotel was in the middle of nowhere, we took the chance to go on a few of the excursions. One day we went into Tunis, the capital, to have a look around the shops and bazaars.

I soon discovered it was not wise to hang around a shop front for long, as on several occasions the owner of a shop would come out and drag you into the back and press himself up against you. They were certainly a randy lot.

The only good thing I got from Tunis was some painkillers. For some reason I was plagued with migraine-type headaches on that holiday.

We went on a camel safari out into the desert, too. I was used to riding horses, but camels were a different kettle of fish. We were given the opportunity to dress up in robes to look the part. My friend didn't fancy putting the robes on, but she did in the end, I am always up for some fun, so we joined in and got dressed up. I enjoyed that day.

One excursion we went on lasted a few days, as it was quite a long coach journey. We stopped enroute to look at the salt lakes, then continued to our destination. Along the route we saw caves that were occupied by troglodytes, but what amazed me was that above the caves were aerials. When we arrived at our destination, our accommodation was in the hotel Les Berberes in Matmatat-Al-Qadimal. Our evening meal was in a cave, which was a bit too smelly for me. I came down with a migraine that evening and had to stay in bed. I didn't see any of the rest of that trip, but it was probably due to spending too much time on the coach.

Back at the hotel, there wasn't much to do. Well, nothing really; no entertainment provided. We had a pack of cards, so we played with those. Then my friend got sick – apparently, on a trip out, she had been eating berries she found growing along the road. So, then she was confined to bed. I got friendly with a young family who were having a go at a 'wacky baccy' pipe, so I joined in. It gave us a giggle.

We were both glad, I think, when it was time to go home. Our flight home was fine, and we arrived in dull, grey, foggy Manchester, but still glad to be back.

Christmas 1994, I set off on another adventure. I had heard so many people say how brilliant Christmas holidays were in hotels, so I thought I would give it a try myself. I booked through Alpha Coaches to go to Dunoon in Scotland for four days. And I have to say how brilliant this company was, they couldn't do enough for you.

I was picked up in our local town, before the coach meandered through various towns along the route, picking up people. We then headed to a car park where other coaches were waiting for us. It was all very well organised, as we were shown to our relevant coaches taking us to our different destinations. I was going to Scotland, so off we went. The journey towards Scotland was good, with nice scenery, but the closer we got to our destination the weather turned snowier.

We reached the ferry terminal and the coach was loaded onto a ferry to take us across the river Clyde, which was only a short journey. Once back on land, we soon arrived at The Selborne Hotel, which had great views across the Clyde. The hotel was average sized, just under 100 rooms. Part of it had been refurbished, but most of the rooms still required decorating for the new season. Guess who got one of the nice clean new rooms. I did. It was only a single room and in a separate annex, so although everything in the room was new, I was on my own. But I didn't mind that.

During our stay, we should have gone on a couple of tours, but it had snowed heavily so the driver said it was too dangerous to go up steep hills in the icy conditions. We didn't mind; better to be safe than sorry.

At dinner the first night, I was seated on a table with two couples and one other single lady. We chatted and got on well, so we tended to stick together. Because of the weather, we were somewhat trapped in the hotel, but we did go out for strolls each morning – all six of us – stopping off at pubs we came across to have a drink. It was a very leisurely few days.

The lounge areas in the hotel were laid out well. There was a large lounge fitted out with comfy armchairs, along with several alcoves fitted with tables and comfy chairs. We tended to get one of those so we could sit and chat, and the drink flowed. Not being a big drinker, I can't believe how much I got through in those few days.

All the other guests appeared to be in their groups, or couples, and tended not to mix with anyone else. Most were in the middle-aged group, apart from three young women who never spoke to anyone else.

All the meals were very good and there was plenty of food. One evening during our dinner, it was my turn to buy a round. We ordered two bottles of wine a time, so I went to the bar to order some. One of the waiters followed me back to our table, with the two bottles on a tray, but he tripped on something. My friends told me afterwards that it was like a comedy sketch as he tried to regain his balance and not let the tray and bottles fall on top of me. I wish I had seen that.

I hadn't really noticed just how much wine we drank that evening. Apparently (we found this out later), the other diners wouldn't get up and leave the dining room till we had. They thought that we would all be drunk, but they were disappointed, because we had eaten so much the wine had no effect.

There must have been some entertainment put on in the evenings, but my memory can't recall what. One night, though, we had to wear fancy dress. I wasn't aware of this, so I hadn't taken any fancy clothes with me, but as it turned out, nor had anyone else, apart from the three young women. The six of us didn't bother with that; we got cosy in our alcove with a few drinks and talked the night away.

It now seems surreal, but as we chatted, we all talked about personal things and difficult times in our lives – something I would never do at home or with friends. It was like a counselling session, when I look back. It didn't matter what we said, though, we weren't going to see each other again.

I was very grateful for my five friends. If they had not been on the same holiday, I would have been very lonely, as I don't recall anyone else speaking to us much. But I had never consumed so much alcohol before that break, or after. Nowadays, I don't drink at all.

On the fourth day, we said our goodbye to one couple, who were not on our coach. They had travelled up from the south of England. We headed back onto the ferry across to the mainland, then home. I really enjoyed that break, as it was so relaxing. With my batteries now fully charged, I was ready for whatever the world decided to throw at me. I have to say it was one of my favourite holidays, and I met some wonderful people who allowed me to join them and accepted me for who I was. I regarded myself very lucky to have booked on this break and met those lovely friends. However, I don't feel I would be so lucky next time, so I wouldn't book another Christmas break. I feel you need to be in either a couple or a group.

The following year in September (1995), I booked myself into a hotel in Blackpool. I hadn't been to see the illuminations for quite some time, and I thought I could do a few shows as well. I drove there and left my car in the hotel car park for the duration of my stay. I think the hotel now is called The Grand, but I believe it has different management now. It wasn't called The Grand when I stayed there.

The hotel catered a lot for businesspeople, so I didn't feel out of place sitting on my own in the dining room. All the meals were buffet-style, which suited me as I am a fussy eater. The food was very good.

My room was on one of the higher floors, which was ideal, as the hotel had a disco on the ground floor which tended to get a bit noisy at night.

I spent the days looking around Blackpool, including the zoo and the park and gardens, which are immaculate and very well kept. I spent one afternoon in the hotel's indoor pool, but I am not a good swimmer. All around the pool were tables with people sitting having a coffee and watching everyone swimming, so it didn't make me feel very comfortable.

I had purchased tickets to a show each evening, but the only one that sticks in my mind was the one at the bottom of the North Pier where I went to see Brian Conley, the comedian. I know what he is like for poking fun at people, so I didn't book a front row seat; I was a few rows back. I noticed on the front row was a lady and her mum, who I used to work with. Brian was picking them out all through the show, but Elsie took it all in good spirit. At the end of the show, Brian came out with a huge bouquet of flowers, asked Elsie up onto the stage, and gave her the flowers. After the show, I headed back to the promenade and caught a tram back to my hotel.

After four days, I checked out of the hotel and drove home, to find a letter on my doormat from a hospital. I had missed an appointment.

It was another six years before I left the UK again. But on the day, I was due to travel, I had an almighty migraine and I just couldn't get out of bed. I rang the travel agent to let them know I wouldn't be on the flight, and I assumed they would let the airline know. But they didn't, so I caused a bit of a hold-up. The same happened apparently at the other end, where the rep held up the coach that was picking me up and spent a lot of time trying to find me. I had some apologizing to do when I did eventually arrive, having lost a couple of days of my holiday.

When I had shaken the migraine off, I rang the airline direct and booked myself on a flight to Pathos, Cyprus. This time, I travelled alone. I decided to go just two weeks before Christmas – not sure why, as that is not really a popular time to go off on holiday. But I did, and it was a bit cheaper. I caught the local Luggabus Taxi on the 7th of December, 1996, to Manchester Airport and it was great as I had the whole bus to myself.

The only seat I could book independently to Pathos was on a Cyprus Airways flight, which was an experience. It looked and felt like a very old plane, and it rattled and shook all the way there, but on the upside, it was only half full, so I had a row of seats to myself. As far as I could see, I was the only non-Cypriot on the plane. I have to say that the food that was provided was nice, and I was impressed. We touched down at 6:20 pm and I then had to find a taxi to take me to my hotel, which was the Cypria Maris. The taxi cost around £7, and I arrived at the hotel at around 7:20pm.

I think I had made a smart move going at that time of year, as the hotel was being decorated up for Christmas. It was a large hotel but there were only a handful of other holidaymakers there at the time, so it was really quiet, and the staff were always on hand if you needed anything. It was also quite warm; you only needed a jacket in the evenings.

On my first day, I had a good look around the hotel and grounds, familiarising myself. I even spent a little time on a lounger by the pool, although that's not really my thing. You could walk into the town or catch the bus for 35 cents, so I hopped on a bus into town and went to the harbour, looked around a castle (75 cents), went in the aquarium and saw some beautiful fish. I decided to walk back to the hotel where I enjoyed a nice evening meal and met Trevor, who had been in Cyprus with other members of a cycling club. All the others had gone home, but he had decided to stay and have another week to relax. After dinner we went for a stroll.

The following day I joined others on a coach trip to Nicosia – the divided city; Turkish Cypriots versus the Greek Cypriots. We were told by our guide that if any one of them crossed the dividing line they would be shot. We stopped off at an Arts and Craft shop, went round St John's Church where we saw some beautiful paintings, and the next stop was the Byzantine Museum. Our guide talked about the Icons of Jesus adorning many of the walls and explained about the flat style of painting, which was a technique from thousands of years. Some were available for purchase, and I have always regretted not buying one, as they were unique. Next stop was the Archaeological Museum with displays of different styles of pottery dating back 3000 years BC, and where we also enjoyed a talk about Greek Mythology and Aphrodite. We stopped in the city centre for lunch, then made our way home past the Presidential Residence.

I was up early next morning and raring to go. I had booked on the Potomas Trek. There were seven of us on this excursion – six Germans and me, which made conversation interesting. Nicos was our guide and driver. We did a lot of driving that day, in a large jeep kind of vehicle with the seats along the sides, so we were sitting facing each other. But we did get three short walks, which was a welcome opportunity to stretch our legs. We stopped off at a monastery, an orange grove, and a goat farm, and enjoyed a typical Cyprian lunch with many courses and free-flowing wine. The food consisted of salad, two types of pork, many sauces, yoghurt, chicken, wild rabbit, with vegetables and bread, corn crisps with syrup, washed down with 60% proof spirit and coffee. The meal lasted two hours; things are so laid back.

We got back to the hotel around 4:30pm, and that evening I had dinner with Trevor and I met Julie.

The next day was more relaxing, as I just went into Pathos town. It was very hot for the time of year.

The hotel was quiet in the evening, as I reckoned most people must have gone home. I had dinner in my room and watched a bit of TV.

The following day, I went into the town, as it was market day, then back to the harbour and shops. I bought a tablecloth, serviettes, and holder, from a market stall. I still have and use them today; the tablecloth has never lost its colour and the embroidery is still as good as new. There isn't a label on the cloth, but I assume it is Egyptian cotton. After the market, I went back to the hotel, had a swim in the indoor pool, then had dinner and packed up, as I had booked to go on a cruise the following day. During the night we had an enormous thunderstorm. Just typical to come and churn up the sea when I was due to sail! I'm not that keen on water at all.

Up bright and early ready for my adventure to Egypt, I got chatting with Julie who had just come back from that trip. They had sailed back during the thunderstorm and endured a very rough crossing. Julie gave me some sea sickness pills just in case. We got ourselves to Limassol and were all ready to board our ship, *Salamis Glory*, but had to wait while a stowaway was removed. Apparently, someone had managed to sneak on board in Egypt and arrived in Cyprus.

Eventually, we set sail. Once out on the open water, it was choppy and the ship was bouncing about on the water. There were two vessels that did these trips. The other ship was smaller, and it had set off, but had to turn back due to the bad weather. Ours carried on and I had a look round the ship before playing a game of Big Time Bingo in the Salaminia Lounge. We had a mandatory Lifeboat Drill before dinner, which was served in the Byzantium Dining Room. We were sat at large round tables, and there must have been about 12 people at each one. It was a bit much for me, as I don't feel comfortable in large groups. Our plates were sliding up and down as the ship rocked.

After dinner I sat in the lounge with a couple, Pat and Nora, who were very kind and befriended me because I was on my own. We watched the Elite Show Girls present their Variety Tonight show in the Salaminia Lounge until 10pm, then went to bed. During the night the weather was rough, and poor Nora was up all night with her head down the loo. I had taken the pill Julie gave me, but whether I would have needed it, I don't know.

We were up at six for breakfast, served in the Byzantium Restaurant. During the night, our ship had been forced to stop at the entrance to the Suez Canal, as there was too much traffic for us to enter. I was sorry this happened at night and I missed it all, as I won't get the opportunity to do that trip again.

Due to the congestion in the Suez, we docked an hour late. We were then ushered into three air-conditioned coaches – two for the English, and one for the Germans. Along the way, our guide was giving out strict instructions about how to keep ourselves safe. We had all been given packed lunches and drinks for the day as we left the ship, so we were told not to eat anything locally while in Egypt. Our guide came down the coach with an order form, asking us if we would like to purchase anything from the jewellers, with our names engraved on. I chose a Khartoush and chain with my name in hieroglyphics. These were made at Ramses Bazaar, Sphinx Square, Giza, and the coach would stop there later for us to collect are items. I still have my Khartoush and its just as nice as the day I bought it. We were told that Egyptian gold was very good. I also bought a lovely pair of gold earrings from a shop in the town in Paphos.

We had a Police escort into Cairo, for our safety, as locals can ambush coaches and rob people. As we travelled along, we followed the Nile for quite a while, which was interesting. We were told that they produce 4 million acres of cotton, along with sugar cane, dates, and rice. (In my scrawled notes from the time, I have also noted that the government gave electricity to all couples at a birth, and rented property stayed at the same price for life, as birth control – if they just had one child.) As we approached Cairo, some of the locals started pelting the coaches with stones and pulling faces at us, but the Police kept us moving through the checkpoints without stopping. Along the side of one of the main roads into Cairo were Police with guns, cocked ready to fire. Our driver on one occasion had to swerve onto the pavement, which was very wide, to avoid the locals running in front of the coach to stop it. The poverty on the outskirts of Cairo was awful to see, and heart-breaking in some ways. The condition of the horses and donkeys pulling carts just reduced you to tears. One donkey had fallen, and it was whipped till it got back onto its feet. So cruel. Once we reached the centre of Cairo, the Police left us.

When we got off the coach, it was a bit of a challenge keeping up with the guide. We had been told to keep moving and not to speak to or buy anything from the locals, who were selling little stuffed camels, pictures of Tutankhamun's mask, and other things. The place was absolutely heaving with tourists, and many guides with their groups, all holding up poles with signs to follow.

Our first visit was to the Egyptian Museum to see King Tutankhamun's mask, coffin, and other items of interest. These were unbelievable, and the gold coffin was stunning. When we bought our entrance ticket, if we had a camera, we had to purchase a ticket which allowed us to take photographs, but the number you could take was limited. It was explained that the flash from the camera could be damaging to the artifacts. We only had half an hour there, so only saw the main pieces.

Back on the coach, we made our way to the Pyramids, which were incredible. We saw three from the outside, but we were allowed inside one of the small ones. To access it, we had to climb down a rope ladder backwards, as it was too steep to go down forwards. Before we all started to climb down like a row of ants, we were asked if we were okay with very small, confined spaces, and everyone said yes. But when we were about halfway down, one woman went into a panic. Apparently, she suffered from claustrophobia, so we all had to climb back up to let her out. Anyway, we did eventually reach the bottom and were allowed to wander about in the chambers. The ceilings were very low and the passages narrow, so you had to walk stooped. At one point I forgot and stood up, smashing my head on the ceiling. I quickly looked around to see if anyone had noticed, but I had got away with that one. The small Pyramids were for the wives' burials, called The Village of the Dead. Each chamber had two rooms – one for the coffin, and the other for the family to enter to mourn the dead. Sadly, nowadays the homeless have started moving in. We didn't have long there either.

From the Pyramids, we went to the Sphinx for a photo shoot only. Due to the statue's poor condition, we were not allowed too close to it, and it was cordoned off. Then we moved on to the bazaar to collect our jewellery. After that, it was back to Port Said again with a Police escort to catch the ship back to Cyprus.

We sailed at 7pm, had dinner in the Byzantium Dining Room at 7:30pm, then I sat in the lounge with Pat and Nora, David and Ann, sharing our experiences and wonders of the Egyptian dynasty, before going to bed at midnight. The weather had improved and we had a smooth journey back. We had a good breakfast the next morning, and docked back at Limassol at 10:30am, so were back at our hotel by midday.

What an incredible day that was, and I am so pleased I booked on this trip. I would recommend it to anyone who goes to Cyprus on holiday.

I spent the afternoon in Paphos. As it was raining, I had a look around the ancient monuments before going back to the hotel for dinner, then bed.

Returning to Paphos, all the pavements had been decorated with Christmas lights, large Santas, and snowmen – not the blown-up, wobbly type, but good solid structures.

On the penultimate day of my holiday, I went into town to have a look around the market, bumped into Pat and Nora twice, and found a little place in the town for lunch. In the afternoon, back at the hotel I had booked myself a massage in the salon. The lady told me I could do to lose some weight. *Do say it how it is, love! She's right, she's right.* The massage was rejuvenating, but I didn't feel like going down for dinner; I was tired, so went to bed early.

My last day, I had a good breakfast, then walked down to the harbour for a last look and was back at the hotel by lunchtime. Sat out on a lounger on the beach for a while, then went to my room and sat on my balcony.

Got ready for dinner. It was a themed night, the food not to my taste, so I packed up my things ready to leave the following day.

Got up the next morning, had a good breakfast, then just lounged around until I was collected at 4:30pm and taken to the airport.

When I got to the check-in desk, I caused a bit of a delay. I handed in my original ticket, but as I hadn't used my arrival one, they queried how I had arrived in the country. Fortunately, I had kept my Cyprus Airways ticket to prove I was in the country legitimately. After the staff had a little chat amongst themselves, I was allowed to continue on my homeward journey. The flight back to Manchester was smooth, but what I wasn't keen on was how we were all squashed in like sardines, unlike the flight out.

Upon arrival at Manchester, I had to ring Luggabus and ask for my taxi, which took a while for it to arrive. I had been expecting it to be waiting for me. I got home eventually.

CHAPTER 6

WORKING THE
TWILIGHT SHIFT

It was okay working a full-time job during the day, but I tended to come home and sit and watch the TV when I was in-between boyfriends or friends to go out with. For a young single woman, life was beginning to get a bit boring. I wanted to buy myself a car, so I decided to look for an extra part-time job to bring in some more cash.

Also, when I was at home with Mother and Richard, I was made to sit in the lounge with them and watch TV, as apparently, if I went up to my room, I was wasting electricity. Richard liked football – in fact, all sport – and it was painful for me to have to watch all this when I couldn't stand it.

I would have to look for a job during the weekends preferably, so I scoured the local paper for any vacancies. I came across an advert for a waitress in the Sundowner NightSpot, which was part of the Kingsway Casino at the time. I had never worked in a bar or nightclub before and, in fact, I had never even been in a nightclub socially before. I thought to myself, why not give it a try?

I rang up and got myself an interview with the manager and went along having no idea what to expect at all. During the interview I was told I would need to wear a uniform – a Bunny Girl outfit. I think I was told this just to see my reaction, as it turned out he was joking. The girls who worked in the casino in the 1960s did wear Bunny Girl outfits, but our uniform was a pair of satin culotte trousers and a halter neck top, in a choice of either red or purple. The men's uniform was just either a red or purple satin shirt, and they wore their own trousers. Following the interview, I was told there and then I could start, and one of the secretaries brought out some uniforms for me to try on. I chose the purple, as I have never liked myself in anything red, although I do think I did have a red one at some point. I left with an outfit and was due to start the following Friday night.

The nightclub was open on Friday and Saturday nights originally, but over the years they started opening on a Thursday, then when the opening rules for drinking alcohol changed, they also opened on a Sunday with reduced hours. On Sundays we also served hot pot supper, as I think it was part of the rules of being allowed to sell alcohol on a Sunday that we also provided food.

I was trained by a friendly lady who was the supervisor over the waitresses. She was extremely patient with me, as I did struggle. Although we had pens and paper to write down the orders, the drinks and cocktails were not familiar to me at all. I struggled at the bar getting the drinks, then I had a habit of forgetting where the customer was sitting. Food was also served, and I was even less comfortable when I was put on the food ordering. I was left to do this for a few weeks, to see if I got the hang of it, but I never did.

As a result, I was moved to work behind the bar, where I felt a lot more at ease and soon settled into the role. I was initially put behind the main bar, where the other barman and colleague was an old hand at the job; he had done it for years. We soon developed a solid routine of working a busy bar together. The best part for me was the till. I am no good at totting up figures in my head, but the buttons on the till were labelled with a drink name, so no maths was needed – apart from giving out change, of course.

We were required to go into work early to stock up the bar and set up the trays with sliced lemons and cherries, and that gave us a chance to chat and get to know one another, because when the doors opened, we soon got very busy and there was no time for chatting until the club closed at 2am.

When I first started work there, we had a live group, who were local lads, playing all the music and singing. The club was very popular and was full every night. There was a small dance floor with the disco lights above it, and chairs and tables were set all around the dance floor.

When the live group left, we got a DJ playing records, which seemed to work well, and the music was not quite as loud as the live group was.

All this was like a fun night out for me. I didn't see it as work, more like socialising with friends. It was hard work, but I had youth on my side and I coped well with the hours.

We didn't drink while we were working; we didn't have the time, actually.

After a while I was moved to work with another barmaid in a small corner bar. We got on very well and had a laugh, as we were not so much in full view as the main bar was. Some nights I would find myself running this bar on my own.

The casino downstairs didn't sell alcohol, so on the nights that it was open, the customers would come up to our bars for their drinks and would wander up and down all night. I have to say, they were really good to us, very generous and treated us well, especially if they had a good night in the Casino. There was one regular group of young men who would come to our bar. I remember one of them wore a bright blue suit, white frilly shirt and dicky bow, had striking black hair that was always swept back off his face. I thought he was so handsome and smart. Sometimes he wore a bright maroon suit. I loved the nights when I worked the corner bar on my own, as I got a nice boost to my wages.

On normal nights, the tips were not that good, apart from Christmas and Valentine's night. I loved Christmas because we could get in the party spirit along with the customers.

Another customer who I remember, owned a garage not far from where I used to work. He would chat me up, always asking me out on dates, but I had got it into my head that he was married. On one occasion he came into the bar with a young woman and introduced her to me as his girlfriend. He was still chatting me up and trying to prove to me he wasn't married. He gave up eventually.

When the club closed at 2am, we had to start cleaning the bar areas, take all the empties out to the skip and just generally clean up. We had a cleaner who would come in and she cleaned the floor of the club and the toilets.

The boss would always treat us if we had had a particularly good night and the takings were up considerably. There was a lady who cooked all the food, and she would prepare us something to eat, so we would sit around chatting, eating and drinking. Some nights it would be around 5am before I left – usually a Saturday night, as Thursday and Friday some of us had day jobs to go to. I have to admit, some of these nights could get a bit silly, but they were fun, nonetheless. On the odd occasion we would all pile into the Marine club which was just around the corner.

At the time I had a white Mini, which was less than reliable, and on my way home one night, driving along the back road home, it stuttered to a halt. I knew the engine would not start again while it was hot, so I had to sit in my car till the engine cooled down before I could restart it. While I was sitting there, a police car went past me in the opposite direction. I held my breath, in case he stopped to see what the problem was, as I may have had a drink.

One year, our boss hired a coach and took us all out to the Lake District; I think it may have been Ambleside. From my photos of the day, it didn't look warm, as we all had our coats, waterproofs, and umbrellas. We spent quite a bit of time eating and drinking in every establishment we came across.

Around the early eighties, our boss at the time moved his business interests from the Kingsway and took over a wine bar and restaurant in the town centre, so he moved his bar staff over to work in there. I worked upstairs in the wine bar, which was a small cosy place compared to the Sundowner and had a completely different kind of customer. We had shorter opening hours, which was welcome, as working full-time and also doing evening work was starting to tell on me. I recall, during one of my week's holidays from the day job, I worked in the restaurant full-time because they were short staffed. Never again, I was shattered at the end of it.

Over the eight years I did bar work – six at the Sundowner and two at the wine bar – all the other staff were great and we got on like a very happy family. The thing was, most of us had day jobs, so we all worked there because we wanted to, not because we had to, which makes such a difference. Many different waitresses came and went at the Sundowner, but the bar staff remained constant. I loved working there, and it was probably one of the happiest times in my life. When I left, the rest of the staff clubbed together and bought me a gorgeous Beswick horse ornament, which still stands proudly on my sideboard today.

I would like to introduce you to Lucy Watkinson, (as I feel she deserves a mention), who later became known as 'Rabbit Lucy'. If it wasn't for her, we would not have had the lovely building the Kingsway, and I wouldn't have had six happy years working there.

Lucy was born in our town in 1872, having lived around there for most of her life. In her adult life, Lucy was a very determined and energetic lady, admired and respected by many. The Beatles had 'Eleanor Rigby' but the Kingsway owner had earned the affectionate name of 'Rabbit Lucy' from her time hawking rabbits and skins around the streets of our town on her donkey cart. At some point she had become an expert at skinning and gutting rabbits. This was a true rags-to-riches tale of a hard-working woman who, from humble beginnings, clawed her way up the social ladder, making money from shrewd investments and business deals. At 60 years of age, she realised her dream of having a three-storey building built to accommodate a swish café and dance hall. Later, this three-storey building was to become the Kingsway Casino. Lucy may have got the name 'Kingsway' from an area by the same name around where she used to live. At the time she had the Kingsway built, she lived in a luxurious Victorian Villa on the promenade and had certainly come a long way. Legend has it that her memory lives on, as she haunted the Kingsway building after her death at the age of 81. The lady I worked with in the corner bar and the bars manager had both seen her ghostly figure wandering about.

Joe Ruane came to Southport in 1949. he started off in the entertainment business in 1960 when he leased the top two floors of the Kingsway Club from the owner, Mrs Evelyn Ormerod, (Lucy Watkinson's daughter) who continued to run the café from the ground floor.

The first floor had a roulette table and a three-piece band. The second floor Joe opened as The Marine Club offering diverse acts as wrestling, bingo and cabaret, with artists like Tom O'Connor. On a Monday night, they held a Beat Night featuring Merseybeat groups like Gerry & The Pacemakers and The Beatles who played there in 1962 and were paid the princely sum of £8.

There were also links to the Kray twins, through one of the former owners of the Kingsway.

When Mrs Ormerod sold the Kingsway to John James in 1964, Joe took over a car showroom down the road just around the corner from the Kingsway. The building had previously housed Madame Tussaud's Waxworks.

Still called The Marine Club, the venture was a success from the start, the club put on cabaret acts with a disco upstairs. Many local people met their future partners at the Marine Club and Joe was a well-respected figure in clubland.

I have been lucky to have found Joe Ruane's son Mike, who shared some of his and his father's memories with me, from a wonderful scrap book they have compiled over the years, Mike has given me a photo of the Beatles poster from 1962.

Sadly, years later the businesses within the Kingsway building closed. After a few years of the building standing empty, it was burnt to the ground by arsonists. On the 6th September 2010, people gathered to watch the building burn, as the emergency services attempted to save it. Very sad day for many people. Poor Lucy.

CHAPTER 7

THE DANCING YEARS

I have had two passions in life – one of them is dancing. From an early age I watched 'Come Dancing' on the television, along with all my family. In those days, the ladies wore long flowing gowns as they waltzed around the floor, and most of what I can remember was more ballroom and sequence dancing, not the raunchier Latin they do today.

I wasn't to take my first tentative steps onto the dance floor until later in my life when I joined the beginners' class at Dancers Dance Studio in Preston. It was a lovely school, had a good dance floor of decent size, with tables and chairs all around the sides, a small bar in one corner, the music system and record tables in the middle, and toilets in the other corner.

The school also had its own dance team which competed around the country, mostly dancing sequence type routines, and trained by the wife of the owner of the school.

I went along although I didn't have a partner. In one way that makes it very difficult to get into any rhythm of dance, as you are always dancing with a different person – usually one of the 'helpers' who join each class to dance with single people. The 'helpers' were mostly members of the dance team from the school, so they tended to be really good.

They held three classes during the evening. The first one would be the intermediate class, so all of us beginners sat at the tables round the dance floor watching them, trying to pick up some tips. Next class was ours, the beginners. On my first lesson, we learned the Square Tango, which apparently is the easiest dance to learn. If we did learn a dance during the very first lesson, it was an encouragement to continue.

In our class were a few couples, and it was obvious to see that the wife had persuaded the husband to come along, as the men were not interested at all. It was quite funny to watch.

After our class finished, it was the turn of the advanced class. In that class was a young man who was very overweight. When I first saw him, I thought to myself: *What on earth will he be like?* But to my shame now, boy could he move. He was fantastic at Latin and had rhythm running right through his body.

I steadily improved my Latin and Ballroom dancing, and I decided to start taking my Medals. The Dancing Association at this school was The British Association of Teachers of Dancing, and I got a Bronze in Latin and Ballroom Highly Commended. But I didn't continue for some reason. I really loved this school, especially dancing the Rhumba to Elton John's *Sacrifice* and the Bossa Nova to *Mississippi*. The waltz was another of my favourites.

I always like to have a project on the go; something to get my teeth into. At the dancing school, when they put on a special evening, they usually held a raffle. So, I decided I would ask around some companies for donations of items as raffle prizes. I did quite well, and the items were gratefully received.

There was an elderly chap, Ernie, who came to all the classes and had regular partners in most of them. There were quite a few single females who came to the school, and eventually our dance teacher asked Ernie if he would partner me, which he was happy to do.

I was in my early forties at the time and Ernie was 72. Despite the age gap, we hit it off as friends, as we both had a daft sense of humour. He had lost his wife a few years earlier to cancer, had five children – all girls, I think – and he seemed to take me under his wing. On one occasion he said to me, 'I have five children. One more won't make much difference.' I think he would have adopted me, as I seemed to go aimlessly through life with no particular life plan. He was a lovely man and was so much a father figure to me, something I had never had.

Before Ernie retired from work, he had been a driving instructor, and at one point he was an examiner for bus drivers. On one occasion, they had been trying to teach a young white man to drive a bus, but when it came to taking his test, a coloured chap turned up to take the test for him – as if they wouldn't notice. Ernie told me that people would try anything on to get a licence. He also told me that all driving instructors carry a spare pair of underpants – something I had heard said before. I had thought it was a joke, but apparently not. Then he progressed to work with the Police, training officers to drive and teaching them to ride motorbikes. Eventually he became a driving examiner in the Police.

He was mad about cars and drove a gorgeous one. The make escapes me, but it looked on the outside a bit like a Rolls-Royce. The interior was very luxurious, with maroon velvet-type upholstery, each seat had lovely, padded armrests and the inside of the doors and dashboard was cream leather. He was fanatical about keeping it clean, and all the engine under the bonnet was gold lacquered, which I'd never seen before. One day Ernie picked me up and we had a drive out to Blackpool – his favourite haunt. When he drove into a car park, there was one small space, which he started reversing into. I thought: *Crikey, you'll never get it into this space!* But with a bit of manoeuvring, he did; he also had an audience gather, just to see if he could park his car.

During my early forties, I was made redundant, so I decided to take a few months out and enjoy myself. Ernie stepped up, because he was concerned that being out of work might affect me in some way. He started to take me out for days, and we went to some of the other dancing schools he would go to. I only went dancing about twice a week, whereas Ernie was out six nights a week, dancing at various locations.

He introduced me to another Dancing School in Fleetwood and we went there quite regularly. Again, I settled into it and took some medals there as well. The Association at this school was The International Dance Teachers Association, and I took Bronze, Silver, and Gold in both Latin and Ballroom, Highly Commended in them all. I'm not sure why I stopped, as I could have continued with the Gold Bars, which was the next level in the medal table. Peter and Sarah owned that school, and we got to know them quite well.

Another school I attended for a short while was Crown Studios, which I think was in the Liverpool area. This time it was the Allied Dancing Association Ltd, and I got a Gold there in Ballroom; Highly Commended again. I wasn't very keen on that school, as they appeared to specialise in training dancers for competitions more than general classes, so I didn't attend there for long.

I was also taken to Ernie's Friday night school in Blackpool, but I think I only went there once.

Ernie looked after me very well, and now and again he would take my car to the garage and fill up the tank with petrol, as I was out of work. At the age of 72 he still did a bit of work, picking up car parts and delivering them to garages in and around Blackpool. He lived in Thornton Cleveleys, in a lovely bungalow. On one occasion he took me to his home, he panicked when we got to the door, and made me wait till he had gone inside.

I shouted and asked if he was okay.

He replied, 'I won't be a minute.'

After a couple of minutes, he shouted for me to go in.

When I asked what the problem was, he replied, 'I had left my underpants on the maiden. I wanted to move them.' It was just typical of the gentleman he was.

He had a sister Josie, who I met on several occasions. She would come down to his home to do some serious cleaning for him. He was a tease, and when Josie was due to visit, Ernie would go round and put all the pictures hanging on the wall skewwhiff, so as soon as Josie walked in, the first thing she did was straighten them. It amused him a lot. He also hung used tea bags on the line outside when his grandchildren called round and would tell them they had been washed for use again.

Josie told me that she was pleased he had met me and we had become friends, as I could keep my eye on him. At the time I didn't know he had a heart condition. What frightened me was when he had been down south visiting Josie at her home, he would drive there and back alone. He would make it home in a few hours and used to tell me that he liked to see how far he could push the car. He had some kind of cruise control on it, which saved petrol, but don't ask me what that is all about.

One October, I drove to the Halloween Party at Dancers in Preston, dressed as a witch, and received a lot of funny looks from people on the way. My efforts, though, did not win the 'fancy dress' prize. That was awarded to a lady with a 'red devilish tail'. At the end of the party, I made my way back to the car park, which in Avenham is on a slope. To reach my car, I had to go down some steps, and as I stood at the top of the steps, my black dress and cloak blowing in the wind, I looked down and saw three drunken youths attempting to climb up. One looked up and saw a 'witch' standing in the shadows. His facial expression was a picture, and I'm guessing he probably stayed sober for a while after that!

Ernie was a case. One Christmas Eve, he tried to impress me by inviting me out for a meal in the Palm Hotel in Blackpool. Unbeknown to me, Ernie new the hotel manager, so he booked a table for two for a Christmas meal. On arrival, we both sat at the bar having a drink, then made our way into the dining room, where we were seated at a small table for two, tucked away in a corner. After a while, I noticed that the other diners seemed to know one another, as they were all chatting, and they started to give us odd looks. Eventually someone came over and asked Ernie what department we worked in. Apparently, we were gate-crashing a firm's Christmas do! We had even pulled the crackers and were wearing paper hats. (The staff, I think, felt sorry for us, so allowed us to stay).

I was to fall for something similar on New Year's Eve. Ernie asked me out to a function that night, and again it was in a hotel in Blackpool.

We were not having a meal this time, just there for the entertainment. The hotel in question was hosting some live entertainment for the evening for the residents staying there, with a band and a comedian. There was a very small area in front for dancing. So, in we went and wandered around a bit to find a seat. We had just got settled, when a couple of elderly people came up to us and said, 'Those are our seats.' We apologized and moved into some other seats, but the same thing happened. Eventually Ernie had a word with the Manager, who he knew (again), and two stools were brought in for us. It was not a very comfortable or enjoyable night, I have to say.

During our time at Dancers in Preston, we made quite a few friends who we started going out with to other venues to dance. On one occasion we came to my hometown to a dance. We enjoyed the night practising our routines, but come the end of the night, as we were leaving, the owners came up to us and told us not to come back as we were not welcome. Because we had been dancing our routines, we had apparently put their dancers off. Well, there's a first time for everything, including being banned from a dancing school for being too good.

Ernie had his Friday night partner who he danced with at a venue in Blackpool. During one evening there, he collapsed on the dance floor with a heart attack and died instantly. At least he died doing what he loved.

It's wonderful now that 'Strictly Come Dancing' has made it onto our TV screens for the past few years, bringing dancing back into our homes. It's reminiscent of the old days of 'Come Dancing', though now it's in colour so much better.

I also enjoy going to theatres to watch the professionals as they tour around the UK.

CHAPTER 8

FOR THE LOVE OF HORSES

Horses are my other passion in life. From as early as I can remember I have always found them to be beautiful animals, and whenever I have ridden a horse, I always feel very privileged that they allow me on their backs.

Golly, over many years I must have been and tried all the riding schools in my vicinity. They have all been different and offered various approaches to teaching you to ride.

When I was a youngster, my mother could never afford to give me money to have riding lessons. She used to say that paying money just to ride on a horse was a total waste, and she couldn't see any point to it. I also think she was worried that I may have an accident, get hurt, then she would have to look after me.

When I started work at Silverton's, the shop closed on a Tuesday afternoon, so I booked riding lessons at a local school. Strictly speaking, they weren't lessons as such; they were just hacking out on the beach, and all the instruction I got was basically how to stay in the saddle during a trot and canter. I enjoyed it, though, and went there for a few years. I even went to help clean out the stables and yard when I had a week's holiday from my job.

I found another stables in Longridge – a young lady with around six horses, who would let groups of people hire them to go out hacking around the fields. She would, of course, come out with us, as she didn't let us loose on our own. She really loved her horses, and they were quite spoilt. She had one rather large horse, and he had an American cowboy-style saddle and bridle, so everyone wanted to ride him. I only got the chance once. I am of rather small stature, so I mainly got the smaller horses. A rider's weight and height matter when being matched up with a horse, just as much as riding ability, so it's not a good idea to put two novices together. We just used to hack out around the fields and down the quiet back roads.

I was beginning to feel like I needed some better instruction to ride and handle a horse better, so I started having lessons at Sandyford Equestrian Centre. They had a mixed bunch of horses, all different sizes and abilities. Not all the horses belonged to the school, some were liveries, but the owners allowed the school to use them in lessons.

I was very lucky, because I had many falls from horses but only really hurt myself once. We were having a jumping lesson outside one day and I fell off, got my fingers caught up in the reins and fractured one of my middle fingers. It's still crooked to this day. Another time I had quite a nasty fall but didn't actually hurt myself. I was having a private lesson in the indoor school, riding a mare called Libra, which was a horse that would spook at anything. Just as we were going round a corner, a mouse ran out in front of her. She shot up in the air and I was flung off. My legs actually broke through the bottom of the school's wooden wall, which was a bit rotten, and I was nearly knocked out but just a bit dazed.

I went there for quite some time. Progress was slow, as they seemed to tailor the lessons to include a lot of jumping, while I preferred dressage, which we did very little of. In the summer we were outside, but if it was wet, we would be in the indoor school. Riding round and round in circles somehow became monotonous, and I missed the hacking out.

After a little while a lady and her grown-up son came and joined our lessons. I got friendly with Barbara, whose husband was in the military and worked away a lot. We decided the two of us would go pony trekking, so we found a place to go and booked. I can't remember now where it was, but I know it was very hilly driving there. I thought at one point my little car was not going to make it up one of the hills.

It was only a small place – the farmhouse was quite tiny, and they didn't appear to have many horses. We were there for a few days, all of which were wet, with drizzly rain and mist, which was not ideal weather for riding out. We rode mostly on the tracks and paths which surrounded the fields, so we didn't see any of the nice views. There was only the leader, Barbara, and me on the ride.

When we stopped for a packed lunch, I got the job of holding onto all the three horses, while Barbara and the leader sat down to eat theirs and chat each other up. I did start to feel a bit like a gooseberry, but you know what they say about 'three is a crowd'. I struggled to eat my lunch with three other mouths trying to get a bite out of my butty, but there was nowhere to tether them. The following day Barbara and the trekking leader went out together, but I stayed in the farmhouse, as I was suffering with saddle soreness. I had only ridden horses for an hour at a time at riding schools; riding one for a full day was quite a different matter. Also, at the riding school I was going to, I was usually given a small black and white pony to ride. He was a lovely pony, but the saddle they used on him had a broken tree and was mighty uncomfortable to sit on, week after week. Riding on that saddle had taken its toll on my seat bones. I wasn't really sorry when that break came to an end, and we were on our way home.

For my first proper riding holiday, I booked to go to Mount Farm Riding Stables, Penn, Wolverhampton, in 1969. This was to be a lot more enjoyable, as the accommodation was more like a hotel, and my room was perfect with a view out over the countryside and fields of horses in the foreground. Most of the staff lived on site in caravans. My days involved at least one ride out per day, and there were some good bridleways for riding. When we got out into the open grasslands, it was just great for a canter or gallop. The horses all seemed very well behaved and well looked after. The horse I had for the week, Shakespeare, was light brown and quite tall for little ol' me. He was very quiet to ride, a bit slow at times, and needed to be pushed a bit. One memory I have during this week was that all the stable girls and boys were young, so always had radios playing. One of the songs being played became a bit controversial, and eventually the radio stations banned it from being played. One of the girls, Samantha, went into town and bought several copies of this record, including one for me. It was *Wet Dream* by Max Romeo, and I still have it today. I spent some of my free time with the stable girls and boys, as there wasn't much else to do really. It was lovely weather, so we tended to sit around nattering. I had travelled down by train, so I didn't have any transport to take me into the town. It was a very enjoyable week.

I found another establishment, this time to do a dressage course and learn proper stable management. I booked myself a week – well, actually it was five days – at Black Birches Adult School of Riding and Stable Management, Hadnall, Shrewsbury, in September 1981. This was a fabulous place; the main house looked like a stately home, set in its own grounds. Inside the house, where we had our accommodation, most of the walls had wood panelling and the furnishings all matched. There were about eight of us in the group and our rooms were very cosy and warm. What has stuck in my mind is how much I ate over the five days. All three meals were very hearty and typical of what you would expect from a farmhouse. It's amazing how much food you need when you are working hard all day with horses, and we did work hard.

The horses they had were all hand-picked for their calm temperament, as there were so many different people handling them. We were each allocated a horse for the duration of our stay and we were responsible for the horse, under supervision and instruction, of course. This meant getting up early to go and muck out and feed our horse and involved a lot of grooming. My horse, Shannon, was a grey, and unluckily for me he had a habit of weaving, that is rubbing his neck up and down on the top of the stable door. This made a mess of the hair on his neck, which was hard to get clean every day. And we also had to clean all the tack. Once all the hard work was done, we had our breakfast, followed by our first riding lesson. I loved it, as each lesson was just basic riding and dressage. We had two lessons a day and we got a free half day when we all went into Shrewsbury for a mooch around.

During this period, I was really interested in show jumpers and dressage riders. I followed them intently and could from memory tell you many of the riders' names and the horses they rode. One show jumper, Caroline Bradley, rode an enormous grey horse called Tigre. At Black Birches, they had an almost identical horse which they named after Caroline's horse, but only one of the instructors rode that one.

On our last day, we all had to memorise a dressage test and perform it, watched and marked by our instructor. We all did well and came away with a certificate, so it was a very enjoyable few days.

I have always enjoyed watching show jumping on the TV, and decided I would like to go to Hickstead, West Sussex, to watch the professionals live. The annual event, The Hickstead Derby Meeting, is usually held in August over the Bank Holiday weekend at The All England Jumping Course. I found someone who provided accommodation for people who attended these shows and drove all the way down there in my trusty little Austin Allegro car, helped by maps to find my way. Eventually I arrived at the property I was going to call home for the next three days. It was a dormer bungalow, which looked very nice from the outside. I knocked on the door and was greeted by a lady who appeared friendly and welcoming. She showed me around and to my room.

They only provided bed and breakfast, so after I had settled in and had a cuppa and unpacked my case, I asked Beatrice if there was anywhere locally, I could go and get a meal. I was given directions to a small local restaurant further down the road, which sounded good. I was tired after the long drive, so didn't have too far to walk. The restaurant opened at 7pm. I made my way down the road at seven, but although the restaurant had opened its doors, the staff were not ready to serve anyone. They were not used to people arriving so early. I ordered something very simple and quick to prepare then after finishing my meal, I made my way back 'home' and had an early night.

Next morning, I went down for breakfast. It seemed strange just me sitting at quite a large round dining table on my own. Beatrice made my breakfast and as I sat and ate it, there was a bowl in the middle of the table containing a floral display – all artificial flowers and twigs. I was entertained watching a small spider weaving its web in and out of all the stems.

When I was ready to leave, Beatrice's husband appeared. He let me out and gave me instructions to make sure I was back by 10pm, as they went to bed early. I got into my car and drove down to the showground early, keen to make sure I got a parking space. I had purchased a new camera and was eager to try it out.

The showground was huge, and I wandered around to familiarise myself with the layout. During the morning, they ran the novice and intermediate classes, which did not involve many of the top-class riders, just a few who were bringing on young horses.

The main competitions were held in the afternoons, so I got myself a snack and drink then moved into the stands to get a good view. The weather was quite warm, so it was pleasant to sit outside. On the first two days, the qualifying rounds took place. David Vine was commentating and interviewing the riders as they completed their rounds.

After the show had finished, I decided to drive into Brighton to get something to eat. Driving down the A23, I had passed a Little Chef, where a lot of the riders had gone in to dine. It wasn't far and quite a pleasant drive. I drove back to my accommodation, looking forward to the following day.

Up early in the morning, I got showered, dressed, and ready for the day ahead. Beatrice had her own unique way of cleaning. The bathroom walls were painted yellow, and it appeared that she only cleaned the walls up to where she could reach, as about three feet of wall from the ceiling was as black as the ace of spades with a few cobwebs in the corners. I went down into the dining room for breakfast and the little spider was still busy weaving its web among the flower stems.

I'm not sure if there were actually three floors to the property. From the front it looked just like a normal dormer bungalow but looking out of the window into the back garden, the garden was on several levels, so there must have been an entrance below the floor I was on.

I set off but decided to go into Brighton for a mooch round in the morning, instead of watching the qualifying rounds. I went to have a look at the Brighton Pavilion, which is a lovely building, and the surrounding gardens were all laid out with lovely flower beds. I have only just learnt that this was a Royal Palace. I wandered on towards the beach, which was very stony and pebbly – not one for walking on in your bare feet, I wouldn't have thought. Then I found a little café, had a bite to eat, and bought some snacks and a drink to take with me. Back in the car, I made my way back to the showground.

I arrived at the showground in plenty of time for the main event, The Hickstead Derby. This was where the horses had to come down a sloping bank then, as they landed on the ground, had one stride then jumped a fence. I managed to get a seat in the stands, right along the entrance where the horses enter and leave the ring, so I had a great view of all the riders as they stood on the balcony watching each other do their rounds. David Vine was busy chatting to them.

At the time I was a fan of Eddie Macken (it used to be Harvey Smith). Eddie and his horse Boomerang were in the Derby, which he had won three times. If he won it again, he got to keep the trophy. He won it!

Afterwards, I made my way out of the stands to mingle with the riders, and I managed to get several autographs.

I went back to the car and decided to drive into Brighton to get something to eat. It was only a few miles and a straight road in; easy, really. I parked up and went in a café had some tea. I had another wander round and came across The Theatre Royal, where John Inman was starring in a play. It was either *The Importance of being Earnest* or *Charlie's Aunt*.

I wandered up to the booking desk, bought a ticket, then took my seat in the auditorium. I have always liked John Inman, so knew we were in for a good laugh. As expected, John had the audience splitting their sides laughing. I'm not sure how the other actors coped, as I am sure he was adlibbing most of the time, but it was hilarious, a really good evening. As we all left the theatre, I decided to wait at the stage door and try and get John's autograph. Two other young women came and joined me, and eventually John appeared. He wobbled out of the door, went straight to the women, and linked arms with them, then he said, 'Let's go and have a drink.' As they started to move away, John turned round and invited me to join them. I would have loved to, as I imagine that would have been an experience drinking with John Inman, but I politely declined. I never got his autograph either. I glanced down at my watch: just gone midnight! Oh dear, would I get into my accommodation tonight? I didn't care if I had to sleep in the car; I'd had a great evening.

I drove back to the bungalow to find it was all in darkness. I tentatively knocked on the door and eventually Beatrice's husband opened the door, wearing the skimpiest dressing gown and a pair of slippers. He let me in and I walked in the dark straight to my room while he locked the front door. When you are somewhere in the dark, and you pass a room that is lit, you can't avoid glancing in...so I did. There was Beatrice sitting in the middle of the floor, cross-legged, not a stitch on, facing the doorway, her body of ample proportions all on show. I quickly went into my room and closed the door. When I got back home and to work, I was telling my colleagues about this, and one of them said to me, 'Well, you know what they wanted…a threesome!'"

I didn't get up at the crack of dawn the following morning but had a more leisurely time and went down for breakfast a little later. I only saw Beatrice's husband on the first morning I was there. Whether he went out to work I don't know.

I left for the showground and arrived just before lunchtime, in plenty of time for the final competition: The Grand Prix. These competitions are always exciting as the jumps are big. Winners from these types of rounds can get selected for the Olympics, if they win enough of them as they go around the country to different shows.

The showground closed earlier that day, so I had another quick look around all the stalls in case of any bargains, then bought some food to take back to eat for tea. I didn't feel like driving back into Brighton.

When I had first arrived at my accommodation three days previously, Beatrice had told me that I could treat it as my own home. If I wanted to, she said I could go and watch TV in the lounge. On my last day there, I thought it would be okay to arrive back early. Beatrice let me in and I went up to my room and packed up my things for the journey home the following day. Once that was done, I decided I would go and sit in the lounge. On approaching the lounge, the door was closed, so I knocked, to be polite, and walked in. There was Beatrice flat on her back on the sofa, totally naked, with her husband on top of her. Oh dear! I made a hasty retreat.

I went to Hickstead again the following year in 1979 and booked my accommodation with a different family this time. I chose a farmhouse again, not too far from the showground.

It seemed a tiring drive this time all the way down to West Sussex, and I got terribly lost trying to find the country road and the farmhouse, but eventually I got there.

On arrival, the lady came out and asked me to hide my car out of sight of the farmer who owned the property. Once inside the house, she explained that she was living in the property on her own and was struggling to pay the rent. She had decided to do Bed and Breakfast to make ends meet but said that if the owner of the property got wind of what she was doing, she would be evicted.

I settled myself into my room, which wasn't particularly spotless. There were cobwebs and spiders on the ceiling – not something I am comfortable with at all. In one corner, the ceiling paper was hanging off. But I was only there for a few nights, and I was too tired to do anything about it.

Inside the house was typical of a farmhouse. The furniture was old and of the heavy type, and she had large dressers in the kitchen full of crockery and a huge sideboard in the living room. The old wooden dining table was in the middle of the kitchen.

I had a good night's sleep and woke refreshed, then went down for breakfast, I was served a full English, which was welcome, as it meant I wouldn't need much lunch.

I set off in the car for the showground, which wasn't quite an easy drive out onto the main A23 as it had been the previous year, but I eventually got my bearings. The weather wasn't very nice; it was quite dark, gloomy, and overcast. In fact, it stayed like that for most of the weekend.

The programme for competitions over the weekend followed the same pattern as the previous year, with the smaller classes in the mornings and the main events in the afternoon. It wasn't all that warm to stand around the arena or to sit in one place, so I tended to watch my favourite riders and then have a wander round all the side stalls. I bought an umbrella – one of the large ones – with horses all over it, and in fact I have only just thrown that away all these years later. It gave good service. I also bought a down & feather padded gilet, and I had that for a while too. I wore it for years when I went horse riding, as it was very cosy and warm, until I got too big for it and sent it to a charity shop.

After the main competition, I left the showground and made my way into Brighton to get something to eat. Fortunately, there were quite a few eating places in the town, as I don't really like going into proper restaurants on my own. Then I made my way back to the farmhouse.

When I arrived, I tucked my car out of sight; it was a bright blue one – not one you can easily hide. When I got back inside the farmhouse, the lady was there to greet me, and she introduced me to a couple who had booked in for one night. It was nice to have someone to chat with. They were a middle-aged couple who were on a walking holiday, and we spent a while chatting, as I had been a member of our local walking club when I was in my twenties. After a while, we all retired to bed.

Next morning at breakfast, it was nice having someone to natter to while tucking into some good wholesome food. We then parted ways, the couple heaving rucksacks onto their backs as they headed off on their trek. I got into the car and went back to the showground. Still no sun, and a bit on the chilly side for August.

I stood around the ringside, occasionally moving from jump to jump. The All England Jumping Course was quite a large ring

– nothing like the indoor ones you see on television – so the horses can get quite a canter up in-between the fences. It's nice to have a different viewpoint and photographic opportunity, getting the various angles as the horse jumps the fences. I was impressed with my new camera and got some lovely photos. When Hugo Simon (Austria), riding his horse Sorry, was going down the Derby Bank, he almost jumped off the top. I got a cracking photo of him. Most horses tend to slide a bit down the side of the bank then jump off halfway down. But Hugo had his own unique style of riding. When most riders' upper body stays still, Hugo used to look as though he was riding using his shoulders. He was very entertaining to watch.

When the class finished, I made my way back into Brighton for tea and had another look around the Pavilion; it is really a lovely building. I found somewhere to eat, but sadly, there were no theatre shows on this time. I arrived back at the farmhouse just in nice time to relax for a while before bed.

The lady told me she had a gentleman friend who came round some evenings, and who would be arriving later that night. When he visited, they liked dancing, and she showed me an old gramophone and some old 78 RPM records of the old dance band tunes. I went to bed before he arrived. Later that evening, I did hear some tunes being played, very crackly. I mused, though, where they could dance, as both the kitchen and living room were full of furniture. It must have been the music, but I dozed off.

Next morning, I had breakfast and set off for the last day at the show. I enjoyed a good wander around the stalls, as I love looking at anything horsey and can spend hours doing it.

I went to the arena for the final competition, The Grand Prix, which is always exciting as the jumps are big. Then I grabbed some food from a stall and made my way back to the farmhouse. I would have liked to have had a good look around the farm. Having been brought up on one, I do like to be around farms and out in the fresh air, but as I had to keep out of sight, this wasn't possible.

I had a leisurely evening and went to bed early, ready for the long drive back home. Next day, I packed up, said my goodbyes to the lady, and set off for home. I really do think it can be a lot more fun going away and travelling alone than actually going away with someone.

It was great driving back in those days as there was not much traffic on the roads; a real pleasure. I did stop off on the way for a comfort break, snack, and a drink, pulling into a roadside café somewhere along my route.

I was still going to a riding school for lessons once a week but had left Sandyford Equestrian Centre and started going to Ashbank Riding School. This was a well-run school, with nice friendly staff and good horses. We had a variety of lessons, hacking out occasionally and lessons in the indoor school or in the outdoor one, depending on the weather. As my lesson was on a Sunday morning, my mother strongly disapproved. She thought I should be at home doing some household chores. I did clean my own room, so what more did she want? She didn't go out to work.

From 1980 to 1982, I took several riding and stable management tests; eight diplomas in all. One lovely pony, a skewbald called Geronimo, was popular with everyone, and I took most of my tests on him. He was ageing a bit and was starting to get stiff joints. When it was decided to offer him for sale, I pondered about it for a while, but someone else snapped him up.

The following year, 1980, I went down to Olympia in London for the Horse of the Year Show. I had booked my accommodation through the BSJA this time (they provided lists of recommended accommodation) and booked in with a couple not far from the arena.

Driving down to London was an experience, as it was a lot busier than driving to Sussex. I think I was on a ring road when there was a hold-up and we sat in a queue of traffic for ages. Then the Police came down the line and turned us all round to go back. When the officer got to me, I asked him if I was on the right road to Olympia. He said, 'Yes, but you're going in the wrong direction!' Just as well he was turning us all around. With more luck than judgement, I found the house I was booked to stay at.

My place to call home for a few days was a mid-terraced house which you approached via some steps and was in a back street not far from Olympia Showground. A middle-aged couple owned this property, which had three storeys. I had a room on the top floor, overlooking the road, which I appreciated, as there always seemed to be some young children around my car. I had parked outside on the road as there was no off-road parking. The accommodation bookings via BSJA were always just bed and breakfast, but I suppose to have an evening meal as well would be difficult, as you're never sure what time you will leave the show.

On this occasion, Maureen, who kept a very clean and tidy house, took pity on me and made me a bit of tea on my first night. It was very welcome and appreciated after my long drive down from Lancashire. Afterwards, I retired early for the night.

Next morning, I had a lovely breakfast to set me up for the day, then set off for the showground. It was only a short distance to drive, and there were lots of different vehicle parking areas, each identified with a letter. I headed for C, parked up, then made my way to the indoor arena. It was the middle of December, so I was glad everything was undercover. Looking back, I must have booked a particular seat when I bought the entrance ticket, as I found myself sitting in the same seat every day next to a couple of ladies who had also booked for the full show.

There was always something going on in the ring during the day. From children on Shetland ponies galloping round a mini–Grand National course, mighty Shires doing formation pulling ploughs, showing classes for the hunters, bare-back riders performing acrobatics whilst riding a team of galloping horses, carriage driving, to some horses doing tricks.

The main events were in the evening. They started moderately, then built up as the days went on with the Puissance on the penultimate night and the Grand Prix to close the show.

I found it very cold sitting in the stands and the seat was not comfortable to sit it for several hours at a time.

I discovered that the events in the ring during the day were the same every day, and even though I love horses, it did start to get a bit monotonous. The ladies who sat next to me said the same. I got up and walked around the trade stalls, then went to look at the horses in their stables and in the collecting ring. As I stood watching some of the horses and riders warm up, a couple of teenage girls came and stood beside me. One looked at a particular horse and said to her friend, 'Hasn't that horse got sexy legs?'

Coming out of the show on the last night, I discovered it had been snowing and the covering on the ground was quite deep. I wandered about trying to find my car and lost my bearings; even the car park letters were all covered in snow and every car was white. I kept wandering about in the freezing snow looking for my car but couldn't find it. I started to worry that it had been stolen. I went and found a car park attendant and asked him for help. I told him the letter of the area I had parked in and he took me straight to it. By that time most people had left, so there was my little car sitting all on its own. Was I relieved!

When I got back to my accommodation, I started feeling a little unwell. A pain had developed in my abdomen and during the night I was vomiting. I was glad to be going home.

The following morning, I set off for home, but the pain was gradually getting worse, and I felt really sick. At one of the services, I came across, I pulled in and parked up. I just sat in the car for a while hoping it would pass and I would feel better, but it didn't. I got out of the car and went and knocked on the window of a car occupied by a middle-aged couple and told them what the problem was, then asked if they could find a policeman. They very kindly did. The man offered me a swig of brandy, but I declined. After a while, a police officer came to my car and I told him how I felt and that I didn't feel it was safe for me to continue on the motorway in so much pain. He called for an ambulance.

I locked the car, got into the ambulance, and was taken to the nearest hospital, somewhere along my route. During the journey, I chatted with the paramedic, who seemed to know exactly what was wrong with me. He told me if I had sucked on a lemon, it would have cured me. I have never heard of that remedy before, nor since. I was taken into A&E and left on a trolley in the corridor for some time. I remember feeling very cold as I was asked by a nurse to remove my jumper while she did some preliminary checks on me. It appeared there was a local rugby match on, as one player after another wandered in with various injuries. I got the impression that they were just going to send me home until I started vomiting again. I was eventually moved into a cubicle, where I was seen by a young doctor, following some unpleasant comments and a rude gesture from the doctor I was admitted to a ward, where I stayed for a few days. I only had my handbag with me. My suitcase was in the boot of my car, which I continued to worry about being left in the service station car park.

Once settled in a bed, a nurse came and gave me an injection into my thigh, through my tights, which apparently put me to sleep for 24 hours. The bay I was in had six beds – four elderly ladies, me, and a young girl in the end bed, who had been waiting eagerly for me to wake up for someone to chat with.

I was told I had a chill and slight infection in my kidneys. This weakness stems back to my childhood days, of living in cold draughty conditions. The consultant I was under was very charming and always had a nice word for the ladies.

I gradually improved and started to eat the meals brought round. One friendly nurse offered to go out in her lunch hour into M&S and buy me a nightie. I gave her some money and she came back with a lovely peach cotton one covered with embroidery anglaise. I had that for years.

A kind elderly lady was in the bed next to me, and she reminded me in some way of my late Aunt Hilda. We chatted a lot, as I have always had empathy with older people. She had already had one leg amputated and was currently in having the other one done. She had recovered but couldn't go home as she lived on her own. One day she asked me if I would go and live with her and look after her, and she would leave me her house and all her money. How sad is that? It made her so vulnerable to unscrupulous people. I do think about her now and again and wonder how she went on.

When I was discharged after three days on the ward, I got a taxi to the service station and thankfully my car was still there. The remainder of my drive home was uneventful, thank goodness.

Reflections on the Olympia show: I think for people just going to watch the show, like me, one or two days is enough.

My only claim to fame, having my photo taken with
Gilly Coman from the TV series Bread. I was at
a works event and Gilly was the special guest.

Black Birches Farm House.

Taking my Dressage test on Shannon at Black Birches.

At Sea World in Florida, by the model of the shark,
Jaws, which I believe was used in the film.

At Disney World with Minnie Mouse.

About to take to the skies in my first time in a helicopter.

With friends at my 40th Birthday party at Dancers.

At the Selborne Hotel, Dunoon, Christmas 1994.
Our friendly group in our usual alcove chatting away
(best therapy session you can have).

Pete Goodall at work in his studio. Photo courtesy
of Pete Goodall.

Pete Goodall, making music. Photo courtesy of Pete Goodall.

The first recording Ken Dodd made.
Photo courtesy of Peter Phillips.

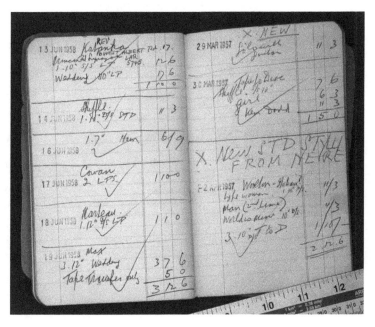

Ken's recording session marked in the log book.
Photo courtesy of Peter Phillips.

Ken and Frank Phillips (Peters dad) in Grandpas Studio in 1957.
Photo courtesy of Peter Phillips.

Julian Molinero, lead singer and guitarist with Medusa.
Photo courtesy of Julian.

Lucy Watkinson fulfilled her dream of having this three-story building called Kingsway Café built in the late 1920's. She opened for business in 1931, ran it as a Café and dance hall, along with her daughter Evelyn. When Lucy died in 1953, Evelyn continued to run the Café from the ground floor, renting out the two upper floors to a local businessman. Following Lucy's death at the age of 81, she is reputed to have haunted the building, being given the nick name 'Rabbit Lucy'. Photo © to Geoff Wright.

In more modern times, The Sundowner
Nightspot occupied the top floor. It was a very popular
discotheque in its day. Photo © to Geoff Wright.

The Sundowner logo on one of the ashtrays brings back
memories, of my short time as a waitress at the
Sundowner, walking round all the tables throughout the
evening emptying the ashtrays, they soon filled up as they
were only small and more people smoked back then.
Happy days! Photo © to Geoff Wright.

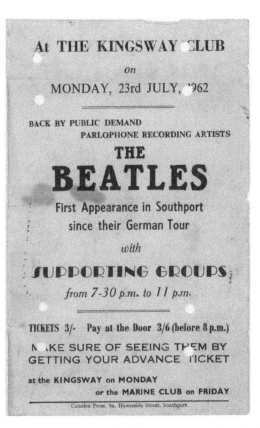

The Beatles poster from 1962 when they played at the
Kingsway. Photo © Mike Ruane.

CHAPTER 9

COMEDY, MUSIC, AND KEN DODD

All our family loved comedy; it was our favourite genre. In the early days, we listened to comedians of the time on the radio. When we got a television, it was wonderful to be able to watch comedy shows. Bob Monkhouse, Jimmy Tarbuck, Morecambe and Wise, Les Dawson, Paul O'Grady, Little and Large, Cannon and Ball, and many more.

Then came along Ken Dodd. He was so different to all the others, and a breath of fresh air. With his protruding teeth and wild hair, he looked like a comedian. Most of the other comedians seem to prefer to stay on television, and I don't recall any of the well-known ones coming round our local theatres to perform their comedy shows. Ken was different, though. He preferred to perform in front of a live audience, as he loved the interaction between him and people in the theatre. He thrived on that and his career was to span nearly 70 years, enthralling people with his clean, funny jokes.

We loved country music, folk, and easy listening. Mum's favourite was Jim Reeves, amongst others. My stepdad wasn't a particular music fan, but he did come with Mum and I to see Roger Whittaker at our local theatre sometime in the 60s or 70s. What a show that was! We had good seats, about four rows from the front, and I was sitting at the end of a row, middle aisle. As Roger sat on his stool by the microphone singing away, many, many times he would look directly at me, as though he was just singing to me personally. I remember Mum kept nudging me. People started turning round and looking at me.

I had not been a fan of opera-type music until I heard Andre Rieu play. I have fallen in love with his music and was lucky enough to go to Manchester Arena to see him live. What a night! I thoroughly enjoyed myself. So sad that the Manchester bombings happened in that theatre a few years later.

I'm always on the lookout for any Ken Dodd memorabilia, and it's great when I come across something. Many years later, I stumbled across one of Ken's cassettes which contained radio recordings of him appearing at our local amateur theatre, The Little Theatre. As this is recorded locally to me, I had to find out more. I soon found myself chatting with one of the stage managers who over time had personally liaised with Ken and put his shows together in our town. He has kindly shared one of his memories with me…

Ken did charity shows at the Little Theatre on a regular basis, raising funds for the Clatterbridge Hospital where his late fiancée, Anita Boutin, was treated. In all, he raised quite a considerable sum. Ken would arrive at the theatre (keeping to his well-known timetable) with his supporting acts (who got little payment). They were Stromboli and a lady who sang. The Great Stromboli, as he would become known, did a fire-eating act where he would blow fire right out over the audience – a nerve-wracking time for any stage manager. Ken would also try out his new scripts during these shows as well. By all accounts, these shows were well attended, and the entry fee was just a few pounds.

I was also fortunate enough to chat with Steve Evans, the Chairman of Radio Clatterbridge, who is happy to share some of his memories...

Ken Dodd had long connections with Clatterbridge Hospital and was invited to become Patron of Radio Clatterbridge in August 2004. Ken said he was tickled pink to be asked to become the first patron of Radio Clatterbridge. The Squire of Knotty Ash had accepted the honorary role after receiving a formal request from the station's committee. Doddy, who had previously recorded messages of goodwill for listeners, said he was 'discomknockerated' by the invitation.

Radio Clatterbridge celebrated Christmas in style in 2005, and the stars came out to help! Liverpool comedian Ken Dodd and New Zealand singer Hayley Westenra had been telling listeners about their festive plans and thoughts about the season.

We broadcast a day of special programmes as the comedian was laid to rest in Liverpool. Radio Clatterbridge announced Doddy Day in memory of patron the late Sir Ken Dodd, and will be giving him an affectionate send-off, with a day of happiness in his honour. Doddy Day will celebrate the humour and music of the respected comedian with clips from some of his most famous performances and some of the singles that even gave The Beatles a run for their money. One of our former volunteers also unearthed an interview he did with Sir Ken during the Knotty Ash Garden fete in about 1984.

The late comedian Sir Ken Dodd helped Radio Clatterbridge win a national award a year after his death. The station won best promotion for its special day commemorating the life and legacy of the Liverpool comic, who was patron of the charity. The official announcement was made by Alan Dedicoat, the BBC broadcaster and patron of the Hospital Broadcasting Association. Committee members picked up the award from the Hospital Broadcasting Association. The station beat stiff competition from Radio Tyneside and Hospital Radio Plymouth, with the judges deciding the Doddy Day trailer was the best of the year 2019.

The Beatles' first interview was recorded just for Radio Clatterbridge. Just weeks after Ringo Starr joined John Lennon, Paul McCartney, and George Harrison to form the final line-up, our listeners became the first in the world to hear from the Fab Four. It was October 27th, 1962, the band was on the verge of taking the world by storm, and our presenter Monty Lister, with assistants, had clinched a world exclusive. The Beatles were playing at Hulme Hall in Port Sunlight, so Monty and his team decided to take their tape recorder along to record an interview with them. At the time, the band were promoting their new single, Love Me Do.

My mother didn't have much money to spend on leisure activities, but she did go and see Ken when he came to our town. She used to go with a friend who was also a keen fan. One of the things you knew if you were a regular at Ken's shows was that during the performance he would interact with individuals. On one occasion when my mother and Frances were in the audience, Ken chose Frances to have a bit of banter with. I think he said to her, 'I see you came on a motorbike.' (Her hair must have been untidy.) She didn't take kindly to that, even though it was only banter, and she never went to any more of his shows.

When my mother married Richard, he also liked Ken, so they continued to go to his shows. I went along with them when Ken came to our town twice a year, in May and November.

At one show, we were sitting near the front and my mother had a thick gold chain, which she wore a lot. During Ken's performance, he spotted my mother, paused and looked at her, and said, 'I see the Lady Mayoress is in tonight.' That tickled my mum.

Another time the three of us had gone with my mother's cousin Stanley and his wife Freda. Again, we had managed to get good seats near the front. Stanley had a very loud laugh. As Ken was on a roll telling his quick-fire, one-liner jokes, Stanley was laughing, but he couldn't keep up with Ken and was laughing at the previous joke. Ken kept pausing and looking at Stanley to let him catch up. That was a fun, brilliant night.

Following the deaths of my mother and Richard, I kept going to see Ken on my own travelling into Liverpool and Blackpool to see his shows. I stayed overnight when I went to Blackpool, but I could get home by taxi from Ken's Liverpool shows. I liked the Liverpool Philharmonic Hall, as it is a small friendly theatre, with plenty of loos and never any queues, which is important when a show only has a short break.

The Grand Theatre in Blackpool is another lovely theatre. Again, it has a small, cosy atmosphere, with ornate décor, whereas the Philharmonic is more modern. During one of my visits to see Ken in Blackpool, I booked a seat close to the front. I suffer from Blepherospasm, a condition that affects the eyes and limits the ability to keep them open, so I tended to sit with my eyes shut listening to Ken. I noticed a pause, and when I opened my eyes, Ken was looking at me. He said, pointing at me, 'I will keep you awake.' I'm not sure if he was a bit cross, but I can't help my eyes.

Ken loved all theatres. Many years ago, when he was younger, he came to our town to play at the Garrick Theatre on our main street. The theatre closed down a few years ago and Mecca Bingo moved in, but due to the Covid pandemic and lockdowns, it sadly closed its doors for good in 2021. The internal structure of the original theatre has not been touched, with only the seats removed to house the bingo tables, so it could easily be converted back into a live theatre. I would like to see this happen and maybe have some kind of commemoration to Ken for all the years he brought 'Happiness' to our town. (In 2022, someone has purchased the Garrick Theatre, and they do intend to refurbish the theatre area and re-open it again, which would be wonderful. I hope this happens.)

During the lockdown in 2020, I started reading books. As all the bookshops were closed at the time, I started searching on the internet for a good book to buy. After a bit of delving into the literary world, I came across a book called *The Dancing Barber* by AC Michael, and I discovered that Ken was mentioned in the book several times. I was intrigued and decided to investigate this further. I decided to contact the author, AC Michael, to ask about the connection with Ken, if any, or whether he was just literally mentioned as a character in the story line. Here's what AC Michael told me:

Sir Ken invited my grandfather, Ostap Buriak (a ballet master and choreographer), to a performance in [possibly the Victoria Hall venue in] Saltaire, a village on the outskirts of Bradford, in the very early 1960s.

He was to present my grandfather with a prize for recent dancing successes.

Unfortunately, Sir Ken had to cancel at the last minute.

But the next day, he went to my grandfather's house with the prize, and stayed for dinner.

Whilst there, Sir Ken introduced himself to my mother Anastasia (who was very young at the time). With his hair 'sticking out in all directions', and his 'wide toothy smile', he quite honestly scared the living daylights out of her! She ran out of the room screaming!

I was also lucky enough to come across a lovely man called Pete Goodall, and whilst we were chatting, he told me about a recording of Ken's very first record, which was available to purchase. I am now the proud owner of a set of CDs which includes two recordings of Ken singing his two favourite songs, *It Is No Secret* (*What God Can Do*) and *Tonight Beloved*.

Pete started playing music at a very young age, and he played in bands in his teens. He is still very much involved in the music scene today.

In the late 50s-early 60s, there were two centres of Rock in Britain – Liverpool and London. Part of the Merseybeat scene in Liverpool, Pete's diaries from the time show that out of nearly 1000 gigs, they played at such places as the King's Rhythm and Blues Club, the Borgia Club, Riverpark, Plaza St. Helen's, Belle Vale Beat Club, The Peppermint Lounge, St. John's Hall, Hope Hall (on following nights with both the Roadrunners and Savva), Litherland Town Hall, Queen's Hall Widnes (on the same bill as Screaming Lord Sutch and his Savages, and Rory Storm), the Majestic (same bill as The Beatles – they learned *Please, Please Me* in the band room), Quaintways, Wigan Empress (Ballroom) – later the home of so-called Northern Soul – the Iron Door, Mardi Gras, and of course the Cavern Club...

Pete was also into the folk scene in Liverpool, appearing at the Philharmonic Hall with the Spinners, playing acoustic guitar. As 'Timothy' (the idea of Bob Wooler, folk and rock promoter and compere of the Cavern Club, and Jim Turner, manager of the Odd Spot club), Pete organised and ran the Sound of Folk club on The Wirral and played at many folk venues across Merseyside, including countless appearances at the Spinners

Club and Liverpool Philharmonic Hall. It was Cliff Hall from the Spinners who introduced Pete to the music of the Carter family and the great Woody Guthrie.

Pete Seager was a frequent visitor to the Spinners Club, as was the young Paul Simon, who was at that time living in London. Indeed, it was the day after Paul sang at the club that, returning to London, he changed trains at Runcorn Station with a 'suitcase and guitar in hand'. And he recorded *Homeward Bound* shortly afterwards, with Tex Makins on bass and the Blue Fames playing the session.

Pete set off with a scholarship to the University of London under his belt 'to pay for the penetration of the music industry'. While at Uni, he was determined to follow Dick's advice, so he went singing in the folk clubs and busking with his girlfriend from Liverpool, Polythene Pam Balmer. During the week, Pam worked as an airline hostess, but at weekends she sang folk songs with Pete at Marble Arch Tube Station.

Pam lived in Macketts Lane in Liverpool, next door-but-one to a certain George Harrison, who was to immortalise her in song as 'Polythene Pam', so-called because of her trendy black-and-white plastic mac.

One day, busking in the subway from Tottenham Court Road tube to Charing Cross Rd, Pete was spotted by a hot-dog seller, who said, 'You're good, why don't you go down to Bunjie's?'

Bunjie's Coffee House was, and indeed still is, a trendy haunt of the Blues and Folk fraternity. Situated in Litchfield Street, it was a haven for acoustic music enthusiasts. Many original singers, songwriters, and musicians hung out there. Pete played there with Terry Masterson and ex-Strawb Tony Pilsen.

Within three weeks, he had a resident Monday spot and had dropped out of university.

Pete was drinking with Tony Pilsen one night at the Britannia pub in Belsize Park when a mutual friend mentioned that a Multimedia group needed a guitarist. Pete phoned the girl who ran the group, Leonie Scott Matthews, was invited to an audition in a house in Hampstead and got the job. So, within a year of arriving in London, he was resident in Bunjie's in the West End on Mondays, and in Hampstead on Thursdays.

The Multimedia group, called Pentameters, are still going strong, employing mime artists, poets, and writers, most of whom are household names.

Pete was invited to become booker for Gale (which was the Tremeloes' agency), where he booked not just the Trems, but the Troggs (which he joined for a couple of years), the Alan Bown Set, Thunderclap Newman (whom he not only joined, but had a No. 1 hit with the fantastic *Something in the Air*), and lots of others.

Pete spent a lot of time at Apple, where he was involved with many of their acts and played with many of the bands at places like the Speakeasy Club, Scotch of St. James, the Experience, and just about every other club and music venue in London.

He was performing at the Speakeasy Club one night when Chuck Berry jumped on stage and said (down the microphone), 'Peter, you ARE rock'n'roll!' Praise indeed!

Pete specialised in visiting Americans, particularly Black ones, as his formative years in the melting pot of Liverpool bore fruit in the music of American Blues, along with the likes of Percy Sledge, Wilson Pickett, and Carl Douglas.

And he is a voluntary adviser for Hereford Music Studios, a not-for-profit organisation, limited by guarantee. His expertise and freely given advice was invaluable to the music studios, the production company Speakeasy Recordings, and several up-and-coming artistes. And he has been instrumental (sorry!) in getting Speakeasy Recordings signed up with One Media and iTunes.

A new 2020 project, this is a Brixton-based event space run by Jos Brient, where he has assembled poets, led by 2019 spoken word winner Uncle Errol, with a group of musicians led by grandson of Percy Phillips, Peter. The project at Azawala is called Nakupenda. The poems and music currently being created reflect the beautiful artwork of Jos Peart, a gifted Jamaican artist who died in 2008 aged 85. Jos' artwork reflects tales of slavery as well as contemporary images.

I was thrilled when Pete introduced me to Peter Phillips, whose grandfather owned the recording studio where Ken recorded these songs. Peter has given me this tribute to include in my book:

When Doddy died in 2018, Britain lost its favourite entertainer and Liverpudlians everywhere were in mourning. Ken had lived an extraordinary life, most of it performing on the stages of theatres all around the country. Early in his life in Knotty Ash, Ken had developed skills as a ventriloquist, and he was a very good singer but of course it was his comedy that became his trademark. Ken loved singing and he made his first ever recording at Percy Phillips' studio in Kensington. Percy knew Ken's family through Ken's father, who ran the local coal yard, and Ken became a regular visitor to the Phillips' family home as a young man, when coal was delivered and batteries were charged at Percy's battery-charging service at the family home at 38 Kensington.

In 1955 Percy opened Liverpool's first recording studio in the living room of the family home, and Ken was one of the first people to make a record there. Percy Phillips loved Ken's singing voice and would enjoy many sessions with Ken and Percy singing together, with Percy's wife Hilda on piano. One day in March 1957, Percy cut Ken's first ever record. With Hilda on piano, Ken sang two of his favourite songs, Tonight Beloved and It Is No Secret onto a fragile ten-inch 78rpm acetate disc. That disc still exists today and is part of the archive of material from Percy's studio that has been kept and preserved by Percy's grandson Peter.

In 2018, Peter released 'The Percy Phillips Studio Collection', on a special edition 10" double vinyl album and a 4CD set. The Collection contains 70 recordings made at the studio between 1955 and 1969, including both sides of Ken's first disc, along with recordings by Billy Fury, The Quarry Men, The Beatles, various local choirs, and other performers, including Percy himself. 'The Percy Phillips Studio Collection' was released in August 2018 at the annual Liverpool Beatles Convention at the Adelphi Hotel in Liverpool. It was intended that Ken Dodd would be the special guest at the event, but sadly he had died earlier in the year and so Lady Anne Dodd did us the honour of attending the event, where she was presented with a specially made gold disc of Ken's first record from Percy's studio.

Ken Dodd was a good friend of the Phillips family and spent many hours with Percy in the studio, and we remember Ken with love as we listen to the recordings he made at the very start of his amazing career.

I had not heard Ken singing Tonight Beloved before, but through my diligent searches I managed to find some sheet music, including the lyrics in Italian and English. However, on Ken recording this song, he was just accompanied by Percy's wife, Hilda Phillips, on the piano. He first sings the song in Italian, then sings it again in English. Listening to this CD, I think Ken's voice sounds so rich and mature for his young age, even though the CD is a little crackly. Considering this song has sat on a disc for the past 60 years, I think I can forgive the odd crackle.

Speaking with Julian, lead singer and guitarist with the Rock/Punk Band Medusa, who originates from the north west of England, he is such a great, friendly young man, who is happy to share a memory with me.

Medusa got asked to play a gig in the back garden for a friend's birthday. Her mother is a close family friend of one of our well-loved celebrities. and it was held at her house in Liverpool. Our bass player Chrissy had made some space cakes for the night's festivities. Earlier we had set up the gear. Sitting in a gazebo, Chrissy took them from his bag and put them onto a plate, about to eat them but went off to answer a mobile phone call. When he came back Johnny was saying how good they were, as he had almost finished one, believing they were part of the buffet. We didn't tell him, and after about an hour, he began acting a little strange.

Later on, Johnny was in a gazebo entertaining people, and put a colander on his head, making people laugh (especially us), then Chrissy went off and cooked a ridiculous amount of food in the kitchen. We noticed Johnny doing a bit of old man dancing during the gig, too.

This is what we want to see happening more often – older people getting involved in amusing incidents and having fun. It's just another day in the life of Medusa, really.

My Tribute to the funniest comedian the UK has ever had.

Sir Ken Dodd – oh my gosh, what a guy!
He's my favourite entertainer, and I'll tell you for why.
With the gift of the gab and a glint in his eye,
He was my favourite comedian until the day that he died.

Born Kenneth Arthur Dodd, he lived his life on the stage
And worked as a travelling salesman, until comedy paid his wage.
With his distinctive buck teeth and a mop of wild hair,
He was an extraordinary gentleman, so wonderful and rare!

He entered the world on the 8th of November, in 1927,
And he lived 'til 2018, when he went up to heaven.
He was 90 when he died, and he lived in the house where he was born.
Floral tributes filled the road and people came and mourned.

One of Liverpool's greatest, born and raised in Knotty Ash,
He put the Diddy Men on the map, and other such balderdash.
He was famous for his tickling stick, and he used it with glee.
He toured 'til his health stopped him, and he liked roses & sweet peas.

He never told mucky jokes, because that wasn't his style,
But he had a Guinness World Record and told them all with a smile.
He was famed for his one-liners, and *Tears* charted at number one,
And he had a whopping 42-week run at the London Palladium.

Pantomimes, TV, radio, nationwide tours; oh yes, he did them all,
But he was equally at home at The Coliseum or playing the town hall.
His signature song was *Happiness*, which was played at every show,
And he had a vast collection of props and outfits, which had to be just so.

He was an avid reader, and the library was his favourite place.
He studied the topic thoroughly, so he touched every base.
He said the secret of his success was simply, 'I love what I do.'
And to everyone that watched him, we loved what he did, too!

© to Nigel Parkinson 2021.

L to R: Dicky Mint; Wee Hamish McDiddy; Nigel Ponsonby
Smallpiece; Mick the Marmaliser; Harry Cott and Little Evan.
These are the original Diddymen Characters created
by Roger Stevenson for the television series.
Roger has kindly given me this copy to include in my book.
© Roger Stevenson Ltd 2020.

CHAPTER 10

GHOSTLY GOINGS-ON!

Since I was a youngster, I appear to have been followed around by spirits. I have always been puzzled why some people can see 'ghosts' when others can't. Other phenomena that only some people experience is when you can feel someone watching you.

One night, while still living at my parents' house, I got up and walked into the lounge. Under the front window was a drop-leaf wooden dining table, and at the time there was a vase of Gladioli in the middle. As I walked into the room, a bright light shone from a corner of the ceiling onto the vase of flowers, but what I saw was not a table but a coffin with a wreath on top. It shook me up a bit, a few weeks later my step-grandfather died. His body was brought home, as was the custom in those days, and he was laid resting till his funeral in the spot where I had the vision.

On another occasion, while in my own home one Saturday, I was busy dusting the fire surround when suddenly in a vision I saw an ambulance come and being driven to next door's house. I saw it as clear as day, and later I found out that my neighbour had suffered a heart attack in the supermarket down the road.

A very good friend of mine died in very tragic circumstances in 2002. Obviously, I was upset and missing her very much.

Before her funeral, I had a visit from her from the spirit world. As I lay in bed trying to get to sleep, I was mulling over the funeral, as I am not a good sleeper at the best of times. I suddenly felt a calmness wash over me, my body felt warm from the inside right from the top of my head right down my whole body, and I drifted off to sleep and had the best night ever. The following day at the wake, I was sitting with another good friend of Carol's. As we ate, we chatted and she told me that Carol had visited her the previous night as well.

On the day of my friend's funeral, we were all in the crematorium, standing up to sing a hymn. I was a few rows back behind her daughter, so had a good view of what was happening in front of me. As I looked at the back of her daughter, who is a tall, slim, teenager, I saw her body shape completely morph into the shape of her mum, who was a bit more rounded. Naturally, I couldn't believe my eyes and just put it down to the fact that I was seeing things. I didn't give it another thought until later at the wake, when a few of us were sat down eating and I heard a lady at the next table to me say to her family, 'Ere did you see the daughter morph into her mother during the service?' Naturally, my ears pricked up. So, I hadn't been seeing things after all; this actually happened. My belief about this is that my friend's spirit did enter her daughter's body.

Sometime later, my friend came back to say her final goodbyes. In life she had always been a very caring person, who would on occasions talk to me about the fact I hadn't settled down and got married. She was concerned about me always being on my own.

On arriving home from work about 6pm one day and opening my front door, I got this overwhelming feeling that someone was inside my home. At first, I thought I had been broken into, so I went through every room in the house expecting to find an intruder, but they were all empty. I carried on with my usual routine of making a meal and doing a few jobs around the house, but this feeling that someone was inside the house with me never went away. In fact, as the evening drew on, the feeling got stronger and stronger. At the time my lounge was in the process of having a make-over, so was empty of any furniture except a TV. There was not a carpet on the floor. Later that evening, while I was watching 'News at Ten' on the TV, I was sitting on a cushion by the fire when suddenly it felt like the walls and ceiling were coming down on top of me and sucking all the air out of the room. Then a black spiral came out of the ceiling in the corner of the room by the door, under a bright light. It looked a bit like a twister that you see during bad weather in the States. When this black spiral hit the floor, my friend appeared as a solid person in the pink shoes which she always wore, although she was in a miniature size and not her normal height. She walked across the lounge towards the kitchen door, moving around where the sofa would normally be. Without looking in my direction at all, she walked straight ahead then, upon reaching the kitchen door, she disappeared. Immediately, all the odd feelings in the house went and everything was back to normal. At no time was I frightened.

I try to be a Christian and, in the past, have been a regular church-goer, but I have always believed since I was young that when we die, if we are not good enough to go to heaven, then our spirits are sent back to earth (which I see as Hell) to live in another human body. My church minister disagrees with me on this, but I feel that I have the proof, and also what has happened to me since my own mother passed away.

My stepdad died in 2008 following heart problems. Most of his life he had been a heavy smoker but had given up five years earlier, following a heart attack. The day before his funeral, on waking I came downstairs and my lounge was filled with cigarette smoke. I remember saying out loud, 'Richard, I see you're smoking again!'

My mother died in 2010 from a stroke, but it wasn't until 2012 when something strange happened. I was in the house and as I walked into the lounge, by the door I saw what I can only describe as a dark cloud or a puff of smoke, which floated towards me as I continued to walk towards it. I felt compelled to keep walking towards it, and when we met it merged into my body like a bolt of lightning. I think this was my mother's spirit, because ever since I have taken on her image, her ailments, and I now 'think' like her, which I didn't before. Out of all my experiences, this is the only one I wish would leave me.

I am beginning to believe that these visitations are the spirits just coming to say goodbye. A pattern is emerging, that they mostly happen the day before a funeral. Except in the case of my mother, as she appears to have come back to stay.

Another belief I have as well is that when spirits visit us, they can only 'see' the surroundings as they were when they died. Like on the occasion when my friend came and the room was empty, but she walked around where the sofa would have been, rather than walking straight towards the kitchen. I believe that is the reason why ghost pictures are depicted either walking above or below the current level of the ground, as they do not have the capabilities to see time as it is.

The following visitation is the most upsetting to me, and the one regret I have in life as I will never forgive myself for letting this happen.

We had the most beautiful dog, Judy, who was a Labrador Retriever cross. My stepfather had chosen her from a litter of quite a few puppies. The breeder didn't really want my stepdad to have that pup, but Richard said, 'I'm having that one, or none.' Soon after, Judy came to live with us. She was a marvellous dog to have around as she grew up, had impeccable manners, was never trained, but walked to heel naturally. She was the best friend and guard dog you could ever have.

If a stranger came to the door, Judy was there. She would place herself in between us and whoever was calling. When I started dating Simon, he would come round some evenings, and we would sit and watch TV. If we larked around a bit, Judy was there, protecting me. She was indeed an angel.

It was generally me who took her out for a walk. One lovely summer's evening, we went out on our usual walk around the fields, along the edge of the sluice. The height of the water level depended on whether the tide was in or out; if the tide was in, it could be quite high, but it never got high enough to overflow the banks.

We were enjoying our stroll in the warm evening sunshine and Judy was close to me, as she wasn't the type of dog that ran off miles in front of you.

Suddenly, a little way out in front of us, I heard a noise in the water and this big black dog appeared. It had scrambled up the sluice bank and just stood on the edge of the bank, snarling and showing its teeth, not moving. It had a lovely black coat which was bone dry. I thought that was a bit strange, especially if it had been swimming in the water. I carried on walking towards it, talking to it, trying to calm it, and Judy was by my side. She just trotted in between me and the 'Beast', almost brushing up against it. She seemed to be completely unaware that it was there, which was very strange for her. I continued to walk on, and once I had passed the 'Beast', I looked back. It just turned around and slid back down the bank, then I heard the plop sound as it jumped into the water and disappeared.

I waited ages for it to surface, to come up for air, but it never did

Months later, in February, I took Judy for her walk to the same location. She was running free as normal, but of course it was dark. Something spooked her and she bolted out onto the main road, where she was hit by someone driving a Mini and was killed instantly. My heart was broken, and to this day I have never forgiven myself or got over that. I had the warning from the 'Beast', but I didn't heed it. My biggest regret is that I betrayed my best friend.

All three of us at home were completely stunned, and my mother and I cried on and off for a year. Judy was eight years old; too young to die.

Recently, I decided to take out a funeral plan, with a local funeral director. I know it's not the best way to pay for a funeral but, being on my own, I didn't have any choice. I have particular wishes that I would like carried out at the time. I chatted with the funeral director (Tony) about which burial ground I want to go in. St Nicolas is our family church and my ancestors and a lot of my friends are buried there. But the graveyard is filling up. Tony advised me to go and look around various burial sites in the area to see which one I like. We have two council cemeteries, one is rather unkept, the other is very exposed and quite open to all the elements. Tony suggested I go and look around the Catholic one, there is a section for non-Catholics. I wasn't keen on that idea but I went and had a look. Its sited next to the Catholic church on a main road. First impression was that it was very dark and gloomy; the graveyard was surrounded by very large mature trees and during the summertime when they are in full leaf made it very dark. I walked in through the gates, started wandering along the various paths looking at headstones and reading inscriptions where I could but most were illegible. As I wandered further into the depths of the graveyard, I started to hear noises, like groaning and wailing. At first, I couldn't make out where they came from. Then I noticed they seemed to come from underground. I looked around and at that time I was the only person in the graveyard as far as I could see, but I was surprised how large it was considering it is in a residential area surrounded by private gardens. I wondered, at first, if the noises could be coming from children messing about in one of the gardens. But actually, I was too far away for that to be the case. It was a calm day, no wind, so it wasn't coming from the trees and I didn't see any vaults either. The noises continued and I started to feel very uncomfortable and felt like I was being told I was not welcome there. I have to say, the non-Catholic area was quite poor compared to the Catholic part with no proper headstones on any of the graves. I turned and started to make my way back to the gate but I lost my bearings a bit as it's a large graveyard. Eventually, I found the gate and was so relieved to be back on the pavement. It goes without saying, I will not be going in there. The next time I met up with Tony, I told him all about this. I expected him to laugh at me but he didn't, he kept quite serious about it. Maybe that is part of their training, to keep a straight face at all times. They must hear some funny stories. He told me a few of what some people want to take with them in their coffins.

In the meantime, the committee at St Nicolas has agreed that they can purchase some extra ground to extend the graveyard for future burials. The ground is on the edge of the village Estate, adjacent to the graveyard, so there will be a garden area between this land and the main burial site. The land currently is being used to graze the estate's many beautiful horses. I couldn't be laid to rest in a more perfect place.

Where I am living now, I had a neighbour's cat come round to see me most days – a lovely cheeky cat. One night, while I lay in bed tossing and turning, a voice came into my head: 'Get up and look through the window.' The voice was so strong that I got up, peeped through the curtains and blinds, and there on the pavement was a tiny little dog, white as snow, and appeared to be on its own. I watched for ages to see if an owner appeared, but no-one came. The tiny dog was just wandering aimlessly along the pavement and I wondered if it had been dumped out of a car.

Out of all the houses in our street, the little dog spotted me peeping through the window. It stopped at first and stared up at me, then it came across the road and walked into my drive. I watched it for a while, but it turned and wandered off down the road. I wish now I had gone downstairs and caught it, but I also wonder if the little dog was another warning to me and will eventually take my neighbour's cat to its death. He is sometimes out at night, roaming around like cats do. I have now stopped letting him into my home in the hope that he will stay more around his own house.

(Update: Over the Christmas period of 2021, the little cat's owner had a chat with me and told me that her cat had been missing for seven weeks. I was as heartbroken as if he was my cat.)

I always know when I have seen something that is not quite right or real. These do come as warnings, but I just need to learn to heed them.

CHAPTER 11

RETIREMENT AND FINDING MY DAD

In 2008 I had had enough of working, being pushed around and socially excluded, so decided to take early retirement. And it's the best thing I have ever done.

However, I had just settled into not having to go to work, when my stepfather had a stroke, which left him with vascular dementia. He needed round-the-clock care, so I did my best to share these duties with my mother, but it was not easy. When he'd had a heart attack in 2003, as we were leaving the house on our way to hospital, I asked my mother if she was coming with us. Her reply was, 'No, I'm not. "Coronation Street" is on.' That just summed her up. She never showed Richard or me any affection at all.

The dementia side of his illness meant that most of the time he wasn't aware of what he was doing, so one of us had to watch him constantly. During the evenings he turned into a 'monster' and would become aggressive, on one occasion knocking my mother to the ground. He would insist we let him go to see his parents, who used to live just around the corner from us, but they had been dead for 20 years. We had the doors locked to stop him getting out and wandering, but he would try to smash the windows to get out, screaming that we were keeping him prisoner.

I soon learnt that it made things better if I put myself into his world instead of trying to keep him in ours. When he was aggressive and wanted to get out of the house, I would bundle him into my car, drive around the block, then return home, and that seemed to settle him. He would then tell my mum he had been to see his parents. Dementia is a terrible illness. He continued to suffer heart problems and was sent into hospital several times.

While he was in hospital, he was so disruptive on the ward and was getting into bed with the other patients. One man, in the bed opposite, was very poorly, but my stepdad insisted on calling him Gladys, as he thought he was his sister-in-law. The poor chap died the following day. He was eventually taken out of the ward at night and put by the nurse's station so they could keep an eye on him.

The doctors wouldn't allow Richard to be discharged back to us, so the hardest thing my mother and I have ever had to do was find a suitable home for him. It was heart-breaking for us both and for him, because at times he was aware of what was going on. My mother was non-committal as usual, so the decision fell onto my shoulders. Once we had decided on a home and told the Doctor, within hours my stepdad was presented at the door of the home in his pyjamas, though we didn't even know that at the time.

After he arrived at the nursing home, he only lived for four days. *A blessing*, I thought. On his last trip into the hospital, he was sat up in the bed and quite perky, his last words to me, 'I'm here to look after you' an hour later he had died.

My mother was so lost on her own, and she only lived another 18 months. During that time, I visited and helped her every day, putting my life and retirement plans on hold.

After she passed away in 2010, I found myself alone. But thankfully I do cope well on my own, prefer my own company.

Once I had recovered from all the stress and clearing out their home, I started to look at what I could do with the rest of my life. I was still mobile and, having my own car, enjoyed days out to other towns and cities. I also started going out to theatres to see live shows – Ken Dodd, in particular, but also to see the professional dancers strutting their stuff at the Liverpool Philharmonic. These outings had been put on hold while looking after my parents.

I noticed I was starting to have problems with my eyes – not my sight but having difficulty keeping my eyelids open. Eventually it got so bad that I had to go to the doctor, I was immediately referred to a neurologist who diagnosed a type of Dystonia called Blepherospasm. Since then, I have been having injections around my eyes to try and control this. Unfortunately, I had to stop driving, so days out were now limited.

But hey! I have my travel pass, so off I go on bus and train.

During the past number of years, I have become very interested in gardening, and in 2019 decided to have my back garden semi-landscaped. I am currently still working on it and doubt it will ever be finished, but gardens never are. They are a living landscape and keep evolving. But it is very enjoyable to do.

In 2020 the world went into lockdown, due to a pandemic caused by the Coronavirus, Covid-19. All businesses closed with the exception of essential services like food and fuel. Medical services shut their doors to the general public, apart from emergencies, so that staff could concentrate on the Covid patients.

These closures sent the public into a frenzy of panic buying and I struggled to get my groceries. This has left an impression on me about people that is less than flattering. I don't think the large supermarkets helped much, by allowing shoppers to clear the shelves of every morsel, but then again, they were making huge profits, so why would they ration food? Eventually, though, they did restrict items to three in any one purchase. I don't like this side of human beings; we have turned into a selfish lot and could learn lessons from our ancestors.

Talking of ancestors, I started to build my family tree on Ancestry, but as I only have my mother's side of my family to go on, it's a bit one-sided.

I also joined a group of people on social media. A lady, who is also creating her family tree has helped me a lot. She also encouraged me to do a DNA test, which hopefully will guide me to other family members. I am secretly hoping that it may give me some clues to who my biological father was.

I was contacted by a lady, Juliet, on Ancestry. As a result of my DNA results, she discovered that we are distant cousins. In my bio I put that I was hoping to find who my real biological father was. As it happens, Juliet was in the same position and had also been looking for her biological father but had found him. It had taken her a while, but she got there in the end. She offered to help me search for mine. After some work going through my DNA results, Juliet found a family that fitted the criteria. In the family were three males – the father and two sons – so it was a case of trying to find which one of those was my father. Sadly, they are all now dead, so there was no-one to ask. This was a much harder task, so I decided to go to a genealogist for help. The guy I found was brilliant at the start, and he agrees with Juliet that we are looking at the right family. I have been so grateful to Juliet as I don't understand how the DNA works, it baffled me somewhat, so her help has been invaluable.

Of the three males who lived to adulthood, the father died before I was born, so that ruled him out. That left the two sons, who both married and had children. One daughter from each is still alive, but neither is willing to take a DNA test for me (at the time of writing) which would confirm which of these men was my father. I have had conversations with both of the daughters but seem to be getting conflicting information about one of the men. It is not going to be easy to progress with this, but I will do my best.

I am slowly finding family members from another branch of this family and having tentative chats with them. I am so glad that their family are friendly and willing to chat.

From the information I got from my mother, it appears that 'my father' didn't treat her very well, so maybe that is the reason that she always had this huge chip on her shoulder regarding me, and her attitude of being 'lumbered' with a child. If only she could have talked about this to me and the rest of the family, I think we would then have had a much more harmonious relationship than we did.

The lesson here for my readers is to talk to people about things. Don't shut it all away, as secrets are not helpful in the long run.

It could take me a long time to finally find out who my father was, so I have decided to have my book published at this point. But during my research so far, revelations I never dreamt of have surfaced. Some are hard to deal with at times, and my confidence has taken a knock, but I know I will bounce back.

ACKNOWLEDGEMENTS

Every effort has been made to acknowledge correctly and contact the copyright holders of material in this book.

I am very grateful to the following people for giving me their memories, photographs and their help and kindness to include in my book. Without them, this book would not be so interesting:

Arnold Gorse	For telling me about Ken's show at our Little Theatre.
Pete Goodall	For telling me all about Ken's first recording at Kensington, Liverpool, and sharing some of his music history and photos.
Peter Phillips	Sharing his memories of Ken's early years, recording his first songs, and photos.
AC Michael	Sharing his mother's memory of meeting Ken. Also, for encouraging me to write my book.
Julian Molinero	Sharing memories of Johnny enjoying a party. Also, for his photo.
Amy at iwantapoem	for writing me the lovely poem all about our Ken to share with my readers.

Geoff Wright	For sharing his knowledge of the history of the Kingsway Casino and Rabbit Lucy. Also, for allowing me to use some of his photographs.
Nigel Parkinson	For the wonderful sketch of Ken with a Poodle.
Roger Stevenson	For the lovely picture of Ken Dodd's Diddymen.
Juliet	For helping me with my family tree.
Steve Evans, Chairman Radio Clatterbridge	For his wonderful memories.
Champion News	For the information about Mr Joe Ruane and Evelyn Ormerod.
Mike Ruane	For the photo of the Beatles Poster from 1962 and for chatting with me about his father and the Kingsway and Marine Club.
WHO	For allowing me to reproduce some of their information about child maltreatment?
Counselling Directory	Allowing me to reproduce some of their information about bullying.
NAPAC	For giving me permission to reproduce some of their literature in my book.

What I would tell my younger self!

Children in or out of school, adults in work, should always live in harmony. A bit of teasing is okay, but when this goes too far, it becomes bullying and hurtful. And then, no, that is *not* okay.

I was bullied relentlessly at school because I was seen as different; I didn't have a father. Today, I imagine this is not so much a reason, as there are many single parents these days. If bullying becomes a problem and you are feeling hurt or stressed, you must tell someone in authority. Do not do what I did and suffer in silence, as this could have long-term affects on your life and health in the future.

I also suffered at the hands of bullies at work. Being excluded from staff meetings, activities, intimidated, and made to feel useless. The women – and yes, they were all women – who bullied me were all my superiors. Again, for a long time I suffered in silence, but in doing so have been left with health issues from all the years of emotional stress. Don't let this happen to you. If it's possible, change school or job. Most importantly, tell someone.

I have been able, to a certain extent, to pigeon-hole all the terrible episodes in my life, including neglect, bullying, and abuse. This, I think, has been achieved through resilience and strength of character. Since about the age of 12, I have more or less brought myself up, so had to have courage and independence. But there have been times in my life where I felt I might crumble and spent many hours crying. But being resilient has always enabled me to recover quickly from the bad times.

Suffering at the hands of bullies has enabled me to gain accurate and deep understanding of people and their behaviours. However, I have not been able to move on with my life, as I feel all this has been my fault. I don't feel worthy of anything or anyone. I have always felt like I am standing on the edge of the world, looking in at everyone else and how they live their lives, always feeling awkward in the company of other humans, never felt that I belong.

I do hope from now on, when it has become easier to talk about difficult topics, that others will not suffer like I have done.

Even today, after all these years, I still live my life mostly behind closed doors.

ACKNOWLEDGEMENTS

The information below is from kind people who are allowing me to reproduce this information in my book. I do hope you find it useful. If needed, do look on their websites or contact them for further advice or help.

I have been very fortunate to have been in contact with the World Health Organization (WHO) who have given me permission to include some of their information here. Hopefully, it will be of help to anyone going through a tough time at present.

Child maltreatment is the abuse and neglect that occurs to children under 18 years of age. It includes all types of physical and/or emotional ill-treatment, sexual abuse, neglect, negligence, and commercial or other exploitation, which results in actual or potential harm to the child's health, survival, development or dignity in the context of a relationship of responsibility, trust or power.

Consequences of maltreatment:

Child maltreatment causes suffering to children and families and can have long-term consequences. Maltreatment causes stress that is associated with disruption in early brain development. Extreme stress and exposure to violence at an early age can impair brain development and damage other parts of the nervous system, as well as the endocrine, circulatory, musculoskeletal, reproductive, respiratory, and immune systems, with lifelong consequences. As such, violence against children can negatively affect cognitive development and results in educational and vocational under-achievement.

Maltreatment (including violent punishment) involves physical, sexual, and psychological/emotional violence; and neglect of infants, children, and adolescents by parents, caregivers, and other authority figures, most often in the home but also in settings such as schools and orphanages.

Bullying (including cyber-bullying) is unwanted aggressive behaviour by another child or group of children who are neither siblings nor in a romantic relationship with the victim. It involves repeated physical, psychological or social harm, and often takes place in schools and other settings where children gather.

Nonetheless, international studies reveal that nearly 3 in 4 children aged 2-4 years regularly suffer physical punishment and/or psychological violence at the hands of parents and caregivers, and 1 in 5 women and 1 in 13 men report having been sexually abused as a child.

Child:

It is important to emphasise that children are the victims and are never to blame for maltreatment. Characteristics of an individual child that may increase the likelihood of being maltreated include:

being either under four years old or an adolescent;
being unwanted, or failing to fulfil the expectations of parents;
having special needs, crying persistently or having abnormal physical features;
having an intellectual disability or neurological disorder;
identifying as or being identified as lesbian, gay, bisexual or transgender.

Parent or caregiver:

Characteristics of a parent or caregiver that may increase the risk of child maltreatment include:

difficulty bonding with a newborn;
not nurturing the child;
having been maltreated themselves as a child;
lacking awareness of child development or having unrealistic expectations;

misusing alcohol or drugs, including during pregnancy;
having low self-esteem;
suffering from poor impulse control.

Prevention:

Preventing and responding to child maltreatment requires a multisectoral approach.

The earlier such interventions occur in children's lives, the greater the benefits to the child (e.g. cognitive development, behavioural, and social competence, educational attainment) and to society (e.g. reduced delinquency and crime).

With thanks to WHO, Information reproduced from the Publication Child Maltreatment. Title: Violence Against Children, Key Facts. Copyright 2020. Other booklets which may help are Handbook 2018 and Inspire – Seven Strategies for ending Violence against Children 2016

www.who.int accessed on 9 March 2022

This does not endorse my book in any way.

We all have mental health. Some of us struggle with mental illness more than others, but taking care of our mental health is something we should all be thinking about. Just like our physical health, we need to be intentional about it, and investing in self-care and self-help is a great way to look after our mental well-being day-to-day.

Here we'll share resources on self-help, self-care, and how to know when it's the right time to seek support from a professional (www.counselling-directory.org.uk).

What is self-help?

Self-help is all about taking our well-being into our own hands. It usually requires a little research and exploration as we look for the right type of help for us. The first step here is self-awareness. The more we get to know ourselves, the better able we'll be to find the right approach for us. Try reflective activities like mood tracking, journaling, and meditation to help you get to know yourself a bit better. What do you enjoy? What feels difficult?

The importance of self-care

While self-help may be something we turn to when we're struggling, self-care is something we should, where possible, work into our daily routines. By regularly carving out space to care for ourselves, we cement our sense of self-worth, reduce stress, and encourage positive mental health.

How do I know if I need professional help?

Self-help and self-care can go a long way in supporting our mental health, but they can only go so far. There may be times in your life when your usual self-help and self-care approaches just don't cut it. If you're feeling overwhelmed, unable to cope, and stuck, you could benefit from speaking to a professional. Counselling can offer a safe environment to explore what's happening and what could help.

If you live with mental illness, regular therapy will likely form part of your self-care routine as you make space for what you need to be well (whatever 'well' looks like for you).

And if you do decide to find help, know that we're here for you. Read our guide to finding the right therapist for you and use our search tool to connect with a therapist.

https://www.counselling-directory.org.uk/self-help.html# theimportanceofselfcare

What is bullying?

Bullying can be defined as repeated and unwanted behaviour with the intent to hurt another person, physically or emotionally. It can take many forms, including verbal threats, physical assault, calling names, gossiping, and cyberbullying.

The legal definition of bullying which specifically relates to someone's age, sex, disability, gender identity, race, religion or belief, pregnancy and maternity or marriage, is harassment. This is against the law.

Bullying may have affected you at an earlier time in your life, but it may have been a factor in developing other issues such as anxiety, depression, or low self-esteem.

Types of bullying

Verbal bullying – This includes calling someone unpleasant names, verbally attacking their appearance, or threatening them with physical violence.

Physical bullying – Physically hurting someone by purposely hitting, kicking, punching, scratching, to cause pain.

Indirect bullying – Ignoring someone, leaving them out of plans, gossiping or spreading rumours behind their backs, or visually attacking them, e.g. threatening looks.

Cyberbullying – Including sexting (unwanted texts of a sexual nature), hacking social media accounts, instant messages, text messages, emails and posts that belittle, hurt or abuse you. Social networking can bring people together, but it can enable bullies to target their victims' homes or places of work.

While this type of bullying is more often used by those of school age, bullying online isn't something that affects only young people and children. For adults, it can exist in the workplace and on personal and professional social media accounts (otherwise known as trolling). Visit our cyberbullying hub for more information.

Experiencing sustained bullying has a serious effect on the mental well-being of its victims. Individuals can become depressed, withdrawn, angry, anxious, or experience insomnia; it can even lead to suicidal thoughts. The first step on the road to recovery is not to suffer in silence, as anonymity is a bully's greatest defence.

Recovering from the emotional damage bullying causes can take time. Victims may carry a sense of shame, anger, or anxiety. Counselling and talking therapies can offer a safe, non-judgemental environment to talk through feelings, process what has happened, and start to heal the psychological scars left behind.

What is counselling?

Counselling falls under the umbrella term 'talking therapies' and allows people to discuss their problems and any difficult feelings they encounter in a safe, confidential environment. The term can mean different things to different people, but in general, it is a process people seek when they want to change something in their lives, or simply explore their thoughts and feelings in more depth.

A counsellor is not there to sit you down and tell you what to do. Instead, they will encourage you to talk about what's bothering you in order to uncover any root causes and identify your specific ways of thinking. The counsellor may then look to create a plan of action to either help you reconcile your issues, or help you to find ways of coping.

What can counselling help with?

Counselling can be useful for anyone who wants to further explore the way they're thinking or feeling, as well as for anyone experiencing a problem or issue they are keen to resolve. People may choose to speak to a counsellor because they feel they cannot speak to their other half/friends/family about such personal issues, or they may simply wish to speak to a professional with an objective viewpoint.

This information was originally published on counselling-directory.org.uk

Please visit their website for further information and advice: www.counselling-directory.org.uk

NAPAC and what they do

NAPAC is the National Association for People Abused in Childhood. We offer support to all adult survivors of any type of abuse in childhood, including physical, sexual, emotional abuse, and neglect.

There are many different types of child abuse, and it exists on a huge scale.

Childhood abuse has many devastating effects. Being survivors doesn't mean that we have to have everything sorted out. Being survivors means we have recognised that we have been through something that should never have happened and we now want to let our wounds heal.

If you were abused in any way as a child, then you have the right to call yourself a survivor. Abuse is the inappropriate, cruel, or dangerous use of power. Adults have power over children, but so do older or stronger children.

All abuse of children is serious and fits into a number of categories, which include:

Physical abuse
Sexual abuse
Emotional or psychological abuse
Neglect
Organised abuse

We should never forget that the perpetrators of abuse are entirely responsible for that abuse.
Abuse is primarily carried out behind closed doors and perpetuated using fear, silence, isolation, embarrassment, shame, and guilt.

People who are abused will often not speak about it for many years.

It's probably the biggest crime we have in this country, but it's also the most secretive. It's a massive problem.

The types of abuse described here happen to countless children on a daily basis within the UK, and given that most of those children survive into adulthood... a question that frequently arises is:

'Why isn't there enough support for abuse survivors?'

The abuse of power by adults to hurt children in any way is disempowering for the child.

NAPAC exists to support survivors in taking that power back.

Abuse is defined as someone using a position of power to cause significant harm. So, if you are still struggling with what happened to you and if the memories of what happened still bring you pain or distress, then sadly you were abused.

Once is too much

At NAPAC, we hear from people who have been abused on a single occasion and are struggling to cope.

We hear from other people who have been abused many times throughout their childhood, who seem to be finding things easier to handle.

There is no hierarchy of abuse. There is no grading of what was better or what was worse.

All abuse is bad, whether it happened once or whether it happened a thousand times – it can leave you feeling equally bad and in need of support.

You may feel you could have stopped it, but child abuse is such a complex and psychological minefield. Saying you could have stopped something with hindsight may seem possible, but the reality is that you probably couldn't.

You couldn't have stopped it because you were a child. They were the adult, and they controlled the power. Children cannot make decisions about abuse; only abusers can do that. They are the ones in control.

They are so much in control that they can very effectively pass the responsibility for their abuse onto their victims. That's why so many of us have kept quiet about it for so long. We have falsely believed it was our fault.

Sexual abuse

Sexual abuse happens when a child is involved in any sexual activity (contact or non-contact), such as:

- Oral sex
- Explicit sexual talk
- Inappropriate kissing
- Showing pornography
- Vaginal or anal penetration
- Lack of privacy to bath or undress
- Exposing sexual organs to the child
- Touching a child's genitals or breasts
- Encouraging a child to touch another's genitals or breasts
- Watching or encouraging children to engage in sexual activities

All abuse is wrong. No child should ever be abused.
Child abuse is never the child's fault. You are not alone

Emotional or psychological abuse

Emotional or psychological abuse happens when children are subjected to psychologically harmful behaviours which cause a child to lose confidence and their sense of self-worth. It is associated with situations of power imbalance. Narcissistic parents may be more interested in their own needs than in the child's needs. Emotional or psychological abuse may include:

- Threats
- Name-calling
- Constant put-downs
- Withholding love and affection
- Frightening and intimidating a child
- Silent treatment/ignoring a child
- Misuse of drugs or alcohol
- Being treated differently from siblings
- Public or private ridicule or humiliation
- Giving conflicting and/or inconsistent messages

Neglect

Neglect happens when the responsible adult fails (beyond constraints imposed by poverty) to adequately provide for the needs of a child.

There are four main areas of neglect: physical, emotional, educational, and medical, including:

- Failure to provide adequate food, clothing, shelter, hygiene, or supervision
- Failure to satisfy a child's normal emotional needs
- Displaying behaviour that damages a child's normal emotional and psychological development
- Failing to see that a child receives proper schooling, either persistent truancy not being addressed or a child being denied an education
- Failing to seek medical care for the child when appropriate

It's never too late to tell

Many people don't talk about the abuse until they're much older.

NAPAC hears from people who are in their sixties, seventies, and even eighties, who have never talked about the abuse before. Please don't feel bad. It's normal to wait many years before disclosing.

Not speaking about it before now was your way of coping. You couldn't have been expected to have spoken sooner.

It's not your responsibility to tell or not to tell.

Being a Survivor

The word 'survivor' can have different connotations in different circumstances, but here at NAPAC 'survivors' are adults who were abused as children. It's not a description that everyone feels comfortable with, but the term 'survivor' has been widely adopted by those of us who have survived childhood abuse. Often people refer to survivors as those that have escaped car crashes, or fires, or airline disasters. The sad fact is that some things happen that should never happen – and anyone who survives such things has the right to call themselves a survivor.

Many of us were quite surprised when we were told we were survivors.

We didn't feel like survivors. Instead, we felt like failures and good-for-nothings. We felt low and we were hurting. We had some good days, but we had a whole load of bad days. We felt like imposters when people called us survivors.

Trust

We know that abuse can make trust difficult, but please trust us when we tell you that you are not alone.

Everyone's experiences are different, and the ways we handle things are different... but in the UK millions of adults have been abused as children over the decades, and many of them feel alone.

Thank you to NAPAC for allowing me to reproduce this information for my readers.

napac.org.uk
Support line 0808 801 0331
Free from landlines and mobiles

"The information reproduced in my book with the kindness and permission of the World Health Organisation, Counselling Directory and NAPAC is for your reference only, and is not the view or opinion of the author of this book."

.

9 781803 812076